the weekend chef
a new approach to everyday cooking

Robin O'Neill

Bristol Publishing Enterprises
San Leandro, California

Printed in Hong Kong

ISBN: 1-55867-228-0

COVER PHOTOGRAPHY: JOHN A. BENSON

ILLUSTRATIONS: MIREILLE BARMANN

COVER DESIGN: FRANK J. PAREDES

FOOD STYLING: SUSAN MASSEY

BACK COVER PHOTOGRAPHY: CAROL M. NEWMAN

contents

and I'd like to thank...

dedication

To Bud and Joy Hodge

acknowledgments

Many thanks to Dona Meilach and Jennifer Newens.
Bullmastiff love to Daisy and Pip.
—Barb Morgenroth

what is a weekend chef?

So you are cleaning as you work, you've just finished peeling 20 Yukon Gold potatoes and you have 30 minutes until dinner should TECHNICALLY be on the table. You quickly plop the potatoes in a kettle of boiling water and take a 10-second breather. Of course, while the potatoes cook you can't forget about the bread baking in the oven...and the sauce...and how will you present all of this? On white plates? Sauce drizzled just so or in a tidy pool underneath the food?

In the kitchen, we all wear different hats. We are prep cook, line cook, saucier, pastry person and executive chef all at once. Fulfilling these roles takes organization. *The Weekend Chef* gives you the necessary skills to make the everyday cooking experience as efficient and exciting as that on the weekend.

what is a weekend chef?

The Weekend Chef is a blueprint to simplify your life. This book intends to broaden your cooking repertoire, while at the same time, minimize the time spent in the kitchen during the week. This is accomplished simply by using pieces of your weekend creations to whip up lively weekday dishes. Planning ahead is an acquired skill, but one that can be easily learned. It is also the key to cooking with ease. There is no reason why the weekday cooking experience should be chaotic or unpleasant. Rather, it should be just as rewarding as a labor-intensive weekend meal.

If the weekend festivities leave you with extra food, it is fair to assume that food will either be wasted, quickly stored and forgotten in the back of the freezer, or looked at grudgingly as "leftovers." The Weekend Chef will show you how to make your cooking efforts go farther while you maintain composure.

what is a weekend chef?

As part of your new strategy, cook twice the quantity of side dishes. The Weekend Chef offers various options for these extracurricular foods. For example, twice the amount of boiled potatoes is a weekday lifeline. Planning ahead can help you decide to mash half and reserve the other half for potato salad or for a batch of home fries or soup.

But it's not necessary to know exactly what you'll be eating for an entire week ahead. Few of us have time for such extreme organization. However, a sense of direction doesn't necessarily have to zap creativity. Remember, as a weekend chef, you will be empowered to open the refrigerator door an hour before dinner is scheduled and know what steps to take in the kitchen. And that takes imagination.

Key to the weekend chef

This sample page identifies the information that appears in each recipe. Use it as a tutorial to explain how The Weekend Chef works.

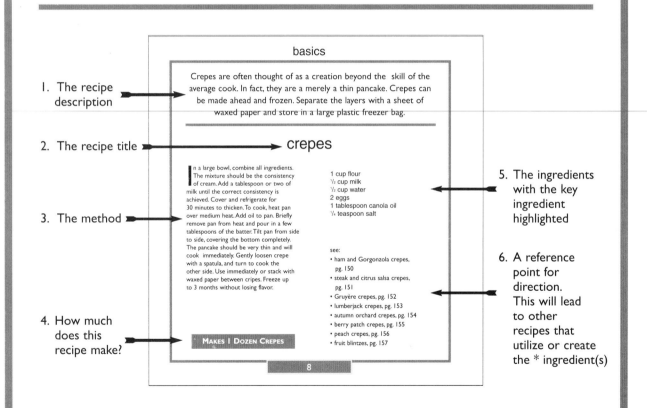

1. The recipe description

2. The recipe title

3. The method

4. How much does this recipe make?

5. The ingredients with the key ingredient highlighted

6. A reference point for direction. This will lead to other recipes that utilize or create the * ingredient(s)

basics

Crepes are often thought of as a creation beyond the skill of the average cook. In fact, they are a merely a thin pancake. Crepes can be made ahead and frozen. Separate the layers with a sheet of waxed paper and store in a large plastic freezer bag.

crepes

In a large bowl, combine all ingredients. The mixture should be the consistency of cream. Add a tablespoon or two of milk until the correct consistency is achieved. Cover and refrigerate for 30 minutes to thicken. To cook, heat pan over medium heat. Add oil to pan. Briefly remove pan from heat and pour in a few tablespoons of the batter. Tilt pan from side to side, covering the bottom completely. The pancake should be very thin and will cook immediately. Gently loosen crepe with a spatula, and turn to cook the other side. Use immediately or stack with waxed paper between crepes. Freeze up to 3 months without losing flavor.

1 cup flour
$1/2$ cup milk
$1/2$ cup water
2 eggs
1 tablespoon canola oil
$1/4$ teaspoon salt

see:
• ham and Gorgonzola crepes, pg. 150
• steak and citrus salsa crepes, pg. 151
• Gruyère crepes, pg. 152
• lumberjack crepes, pg. 153
• autumn orchard crepes, pg. 154
• berry patch crepes, pg. 155
• peach crepes, pg. 156
• fruit blintzes, pg. 157

MAKES 1 DOZEN CREPES

8

Key to the weekend chef

1. A descriptive thought about the recipe. This is a weekend thought when the mind wanders a bit more freely.

2. The recipe title.

3. The method explains how to prepare the recipe.

4. How much does this recipe make?

5. The recipe ingredients are listed in the order they are used. Please take note of the special *.
   This symbol signals that this is the showcased ingredient from the master recipe used to make other recipes.

6. This box directs you to the recipes that utilize or create the showcased (*) ingredient(s).

the basics

The results are worth the time you invest on the weekend. As flour reacts to changing weather conditions and absorbs ambient humidity, adjust the amount of flour.

pizza dough

In a small bowl, add yeast to warm water and sugar. Allow to rest for a few minutes. If you do not see any activity in yeast mixture, yeast is inactive. In that case, open a new packet and begin again. Add olive oil to yeast mixture. Place 1 cup of the flour in a large mixing bowl. Stir well and add salt. Incorporate remaining flour, adding $1/4$ cup increments. When dough pulls away from the sides of bowl, remove and place on a large piece of floured waxed paper.

To knead, push dough away from you with the heels of your hands. Fold dough in half, turning a quarter turn. Continue kneading. Dust with flour when dough becomes sticky. Knead for about 10 minutes until dough is smooth and elastic.

Form dough into ball and place in a large oiled bowl. Cover with a clean dish towel or plastic wrap. Let rise for about 1 hour. When dough has doubled in size, flatten dough and roll out into a circle on a floured surface. The dough can be stored in plastic bags for later use. If you use frozen dough, remove from freezer in the morning and refrigerate to thaw. Remove dough from plastic, flour lightly and punch down. Form into desired shape. You can bake your pizza on a Pyrex pie pan, glass ovenproof pizza plate or cookie sheet.

1 packet or 2 teaspoons
   fast-acting yeast
$3/4$ cup water, warmed to 110°
1 teaspoon sugar
2 tablespoons olive oil
2 $1/2$ - 3 cups bread flour
1 teaspoon salt

SEE:

• Gorgonzola and walnut pizza, pg. 136

• pizza Margherita, pg. 137

• four pepper pizza, pg. 138

• pizza di Parma, pg. 139

• tricoloré pizza, pg. 140

• white pizza, pg. 141

• Crescent City pizza, pg. 142

MAKES 4 SERVINGS

Here's an opportunity for great creativity.
Match a flavored crust to a specific topping. If the topping
has a bit of spice, consider a mild crust for balance.

pizza crusts

A word about toppings

If the topping isn't too hot – like the tame Margherita – an herb crust might be what you are looking for.

Keep color in mind, too. A sun-dried tomato crust will have a red-orange tint. Match that with a topping that doesn't rely on red tomato sauce and the result will be a multicolored masterpiece!

Mozzarella comes in two forms: the solid block is wrapped in heavy plastic and fresh mozzarella is packed in water. Fresh mozzarella is usually found at the deli counter of most supermarkets or in gourmet stores. It is worth the effort to track it down. The taste and melting qualities are far superior to the solid cheese. Slice this delicate cheese – it's not sturdy enough to grate – and allow it to drain on a few layers of paper towels before using.

flavored pizza crusts

sun-dried tomato and basil
If you're using tomatoes in oil, use the oil as a replacement for olive oil in the recipe for added flavor.

2 tablespoons minced sun-dried tomatoes

1 tablespoon minced fresh basil

Add these to the basic dough and proceed with the method.

cornmeal crust
Substitute 1 cup bread flour for 1 cup cornmeal. Mix both together and proceed with the basic recipe.

herb crust
You can use a teaspoon of your fresh herb or herbs of choice. Rosemary, dill or parsley all lend themselves to an excellent pizza crust. Add to the basic dough and proceed with the method.

One may wonder, why bother with the different pasta shapes? It is truly an art to use the correct pasta shape with the right sauce. Certain shapes provide sturdier support for heavier sauces while the more flimsy noodles require lighter coatings.

pasta shapes

Dry pasta on a drying rack or dowel positioned between two chairs.
You may wind the fresh pasta into a nest, wrap it well in a heavy plastic bag and freeze until needed. You may also store fresh pasta in an airtight container for about a week in the refrigerator.

tagliolini:
Dough should be almost paper thin, cut into $1/8$-inch strips.

tagliatelle:
Dough should be almost paper thin, cut into $1/4$-inch strips.

fettuccini:
Dough should be almost paper thin, cut into $1/2$-inch strips.

lasagne:
Dough should be a bit thicker, cut into 1-inch wide strips.

pasta rags (maltagliati):
Lasagne strips are cut into 1-inch squares or triangles.

Fresh pasta is worth the weekend effort.
If you have a pasta machine or food processor, follow the manufacturer's directions. If you have a pasta rolling machine, prepare the dough as follows; follow the manufacturer's directions. And if you're doing it all by hand, follow all these directions!

pasta dough

In a large bowl, mound flour and make a well in center. Add sugar, salt and oil to well. Using a wooden spoon or your hands, gradually incorporate eggs into flour. Mix continuously until completely blended and dough becomes stiff. If dough is too dry, add water. If dough is too sticky, add more flour. Knead until dough is silky smooth, about 5 to 10 minutes. Cover and let rest for at least 30 minutes. Roll out dough either by machine or by hand using a rolling pin, turning dough frequently as you roll it out. Dust surface with flour as needed. Roll dough to an even thickness as use dictates. Let dough rest again for about 5 minutes. Cut into desired shape with a very sharp knife.

3 cups unbleached flour
1 teaspoon sugar
1 teaspoon salt
2 tablespoons olive oil
4 large eggs, beaten
extra water for stiff dough

see:

- salmon pasta salad, pg. 77
- why is it Sicilian pasta? pg. 89
- tomato-pesto gnocchi, pg. 128
- hay and straw pasta, pg. 143
- three pepper pasta, pg. 144
- summer day pasta, pg. 145
- spaghetti, eggs and cheese, pg. 146
- eggplant lasagne, pg. 148
- cold sesame noodles, pg. 149

MAKES 4 SERVINGS

variations on pasta dough

flavored pasta dough

Parmesan pepper pasta
Knead 6 oz. grated Parmesan and 1 teaspoon ground black pepper into pasta dough.

lemon-pepper pasta
Knead 3 tablespoons minced lemon zest and 1 teaspoon ground black pepper into pasta dough.

beet pasta
Knead 3-4 tablespoons grated beet into pasta dough.

wild mushroom pasta
Knead 3-4 tablespoons minced wild mushrooms into pasta dough.

jalapeño pasta
Knead 2-3 jalapeño peppers, seeded and minced, into pasta dough.

spinach pasta
Knead 4 tablespoons minced defrosted frozen spinach, squeezed dry, into pasta dough.

sun-dried tomato pasta
Knead 3-4 tablespoons sun-dried tomato paste into pasta dough.

carrot-dill pasta
Knead 3-4 tablespoons cooked, mashed carrots and 1 teaspoon dill seed into pasta dough.

basil and roasted garlic pasta
Knead 3 tablespoons minced basil and 1-2 tablespoons roasted garlic into pasta dough.

Crepes are often thought of as a creation beyond the skill of the average cook. In fact, they are merely a thin pancake. Crepes can be made ahead and frozen. Separate the layers with sheets of waxed paper and store in a large plastic freezer bag.

crepes

In a large bowl, combine all ingredients. The mixture should be the consistency of cream. Add a tablespoon or two of milk until the correct consistency is achieved. Cover and refrigerate for 30 minutes to thicken. To cook, heat pan over medium heat. Add oil to pan. Briefly remove pan from heat and pour in a few tablespoons of the batter. Tilt pan from side to side, covering the bottom completely. The pancake should be very thin and will cook immediately. Gently loosen crepe with a spatula, and turn to cook the other side. Use immediately or stack with waxed paper between crepes. Freeze up to 3 months without losing flavor.

1 cup flour
$^1/_2$ cup milk
$^1/_2$ cup water
2 eggs
1 tablespoon canola oil
$^1/_4$ teaspoon salt

see:
- ham and Gorgonzola crepes, pg. 150
- steak and citrus salsa crepes, pg. 151
- Gruyère crepes, pg. 152
- lumberjack crepes, pg. 153
- autumn orchard crepes, pg. 154
- berry patch crepes, pg. 155
- peach crepes, pg. 156
- fruit blintzes, pg. 157

MAKES 1 DOZEN CREPES

This is a versatile condiment to have in the refrigerator. It goes especially well with ham, swiped on crusty bread.

honey mustard

Heat all ingredients in a saucepan until sugar has dissolved and mixture has thickened to the consistency of honey.

1 cup dark, raw honey
1 cup Dijon mustard
$1/2$ cup brown sugar, packed
$2/3$ cup cider vinegar
1 teaspoon mustard seeds

see:

- honey-mustard steaks , pg. 42
- honey-mustard glazed ham, pg. 44
- honey-mustard chicken, pg. 45
- honey-mustard chicken pitas, pg. 97
- honey-mustard green beans, pg. 132

MAKES 2 CUPS

Slow cooking brings out the sweetness of the onions.
It is a process that can't be rushed.

sweet onion sauce

In a stockpot, heat oil and add onions. Simmer for about 1 hour, taking care not to burn. If needed, add water to thin. When onions begin to brown, add garlic and sauté. Add remaining ingredients and simmer for another hour, or until reduced and thickened. Season with salt and pepper. May be used on fried polenta squares or pasta or as a topping for pizza.

$1/4$ cup olive oil
6 large onions, thinly sliced
1 tablespoon water, optional
6 cloves garlic, minced
1 tablespoon minced fresh flat-leaf
  parsley
$1/2$ teaspoon minced fresh basil
$1/2$ teaspoon minced fresh rosemary
1 cup chicken stock
1 cup white wine
salt and pepper to taste

see:
• sweet onion chicken, pg. 46

MAKES 3 CUPS

Use this pesto as you would the "standard" pesto.
It is especially good spooned over fried polenta or crostini.

tomato pesto

Rinse basil and parsley thoroughly; dry and place in a blender container. Cut tomatoes into sections and add to blender. Add remaining ingredients and process until well blended but not into a paste. Tomatoes should be slightly chunky. Transfer pesto to an airtight container. Will keep refrigerated for up to 1 week.

$^{1}/_{2}$ cup chopped fresh basil
$^{1}/_{2}$ cup fresh chopped Italian parsley
4 large ripe tomatoes
$^{1}/_{2}$ cup pecorino Romano cheese
$^{1}/_{2}$ cup grated Parmesan cheese
2 cloves garlic, minced
$^{1}/_{2}$ cup pine nuts, toasted
$^{1}/_{4}$ cup olive oil
salt and pepper to taste

see:

• grilled vegetable and tomato pesto wraps, pg. 78
• eggplant lasagne, pg. 148
• tomato pesto gnocchi, pg. 128

MAKES 3 CUPS

This fresh salsa is terrific as a dip, but is equally good spooned over fried polenta or as a marinade for chicken.

tomato salsa

In a medium bowl, combine all ingredients and stir to blend. Cover and refrigerate to blend flavors.

2 cups diced fresh tomatoes
2 jalapeño peppers, ribs and seeds removed, chopped
2 tablespoons chopped fresh cilantro
2 tablespoons lime juice salt and pepper to taste

see:
- duck quesadillas, pg. 73
- a slice or two of fried polenta, pg. 116

MAKES 2 CUPS

Bright and sunny but with an undeniable fire,
this salsa goes well with grilled steak but can be
used as a marinade as well as a dressing.

sunny citrus salsa

Combine all ingredients in a bowl and stir well. Cover and refrigerate for several hours.

6 tangerines, peeled and chopped
1 lemon, peeled and chopped
1 teaspoon grated lemon zest
1 lime, peeled and chopped
1 teaspoon grated lime zest
1/4 cup fresh orange juice
1/2 cup diced red onions
2 jalapeño peppers, seeded and minced
2 tablespoons sugar
2 tablespoons chopped fresh cilantro
1 tablespoon peeled, minced fresh ginger
1/4 cup cider vinegar
salt and pepper to taste

see:
• tuna with citrus salsa, pg 63
• duck quesadillas, pg. 73
• chicken wraps with a whole lot of citrus, pg. 91
• steak and citrus salsa crepes, pg. 151

MAKES 3 CUPS

Once you get a taste of this, you'll wonder
how you got along without it.

plum sauce

Place all ingredients in a blender container. Process briefly to combine. Transfer plum sauce to an airtight container and refrigerate until ready to use.

$^1/_2$ cup apricot jelly
$1^1/_2$ cups plum jelly
2 tablespoons rice wine vinegar
1 tablespoon light soy sauce
$^1/_4$ teaspoon ground ginger
$^1/_8$ teaspoon cayenne pepper

see:
• pork tenderloin, pg. 39
• chicken egg rolls, pg. 51
• glazed duck, pg. 61
• moo shu duck, pg. 72
• grilled tuna roll-ups, pg. 75
• pink loaf, pg. 99
• sweet and sour meatballs, pg. 103

MAKES 2 CUPS

You shouldn't have problems finding ways to use
this dressing during the week.

hail Caesar dressing

In a bowl, whisk to blend garlic, mayonnaise, lemon juice, Parmesan cheese, Worcestershire sauce, anchovy paste and vinegar. Season with salt and pepper. Cover and refrigerate for several hours before use.

3 cloves garlic, minced
$1/2$ cup mayonnaise
$1/3$ cup lemon juice
1 cup grated Parmesan cheese
2 teaspoons Worcestershire sauce
2 teaspoons anchovy paste,
   or to taste
2 tablespoons white wine vinegar
salt and pepper to taste

MAKES 2 CUPS

see:
- Caesar steak salad, pg. 88

Croutons add crunch to salad and are indispensable in soup.

garlic crunch croutons

Heat oven to 350°. In a large bowl, thoroughly combine bread cubes, olive oil, minced garlic and spices. Spread bread evenly on a baking sheet. Bake until golden brown, about 20 minutes. Remove from oven and cool. Serve immediately or store in an airtight container.

* 8 slices leftover peasant bread, cubed, pg. 31
1/4 cup olive oil
3 cloves garlic, minced
salt and black pepper to taste
cayenne pepper to taste

see:
- peasant bread, pg. 31
- Caesar steak salad, pg. 88
- look at the colorful salad, pg. 108
- white bean soup, pg. 119

MAKES 4 CUPS

roasted eggplant

Heat oven to 375°. Cut eggplants in half. Place cut side down in a baking dish. Prick skins with a fork. Bake until soft, about 30 minutes. Remove from oven and let cool. Scoop flesh from eggplants and store in an airtight container.

2 large eggplants

see:

• eggplant casserole, pg. 54

• baba ghanoush, pg. 122

• eggplant lasagne, pg 148

boiled potatoes

In a large pot, boil water and add potatoes. Cook until potatoes are tender, about 15 to 20 minutes Drain potatoes, reserving cooking water.

4 lb. russet potatoes, peeled and quartered

see:

• smashed potatoes, pg. 55

• red flannel hash, pg. 87

• Caesar steak salad, pg. 88

• one potato, two potato soup, pg. 123

• home fries, pg. 125

• bacon potato salad, pg. 127

• anchovy potato salad, pg. 129

Corn is a staple ingredient in parts of Italy; here's a traditional way to use it.

polenta

Grease a loaf pan. In a large saucepan, bring water or milk and salt to a boil. Slowly pour cornmeal in, whisking constantly. Lower heat and continue to whisk until polenta begins to come away from the sides of the pan, about 15 minutes. The mixture should be quite thick when butter is added. Pour into prepared loaf pan and cover with plastic wrap. Refrigerate until very firm. Unmold carefully and cut into $1/2$-inch slices.

3 cups water or milk
$1/2$ teaspoon salt
1 cup coarse ground cornmeal
2 tablespoons butter

MAKES 6 SERVINGS

see:
• a slice or two of fried polenta, pg. 116

Cream is back in vogue. So keep this in mind and indulge. Taking the plunge into something this rich isn't always a punishable offense.

Gorgonzola cream sauce

In a medium saucepan, heat cream and cheese over low heat. Simmer until mixture has reduced and thickened. Remove from heat. Serve half over fettucini; reserve half for a weekday meal.

3 cups heavy cream
1 cup crumbled Gorgonzola cheese
salt and pepper to taste

see:

- hay and straw pasta, pg. 143
- ham and Gorgonzola crepes, pg. 150

MAKES 3 CUPS

This basic spaghetti sauce stores well in the freezer. Remember to make more than enough — it's versatility goes a long way. Raisins add sweetness and tradition found in Sicily.

tomato sauce

Heat oil in a large saucepan. Add onion and sauté slowly until translucent. Add garlic and sauté briefly. Add remaining ingredients and simmer for about 3 hours, adding water periodically when the sauce gets quite thick. Do not let sauce scorch. Remove from heat, reserve half in airtight containers and freeze when cool. Use remainder for lasagne, pizza or pasta.

½ cup extra virgin olive oil
2 carrots, minced
4 cloves garlic, minced
2 cans (28 oz. each) whole tomatoes in puree
2 medium onions, minced
2 tablespoons raisins
2 tablespoons chopped fresh flat-leaf parsley
salt and pepper to taste

MAKES 3 CUPS

see:
• eggplant lasagne, pg. 148

This basic loaf lends itself well to a variety of uses. Don't let the name fool you. The loaf's fine taste is suited for both the peasant and nouveau riche classes.

peasant bread

Heat water. In a small bowl, add yeast and sugar to water. Let stand several minutes to activate. Add oil to yeast mixture. Add 1 cup flour to a large bowl. Pour yeast mixture into flour and stir well with a wooden spoon. Gradually incorporate another cup of flour, stirring well, and add salt, rosemary and olives. Continue adding flour, mixing well, until all flour is used and dough holds together and pulls away from the sides of the bowl. Turn dough onto a floured surface and begin kneading. Knead until dough is silky smooth, about 10 minutes. Place dough in large oiled bowl, cover and let rest in a warm spot for about 90 minutes, or until doubled in size. When dough has doubled, punch it down on a floured surface, removing all air bubbles. Oil a baking sheet and dust with cornmeal. Shape dough into a round, place on baking sheet, cover and let rise until doubled in size, about 40 minutes. Using a sharp knife, cut several diagonal slashes across top of loaf. Heat oven to 425°. Place bread in oven and bake, spritzing loaf with water every 15 minutes. Bake for 40 minutes or until loaf is golden brown. Remove and cool on a wire rack.

1 cup hot water (110°-120°)
$1^1/_2$ teaspoons yeast
1 teaspoon sugar
3-4 cups bread flour
1 tablespoon olive oil
2 teaspoons salt
$^1/_4$ cup black olives, oil-packed, pitted and chopped
1 teaspoon chopped fresh rosemary
1 tablespoon cornmeal

see:
- garlic crunch croutons, pg. 26
- bread soup, pg. 110
- fresh mozzarella crostini, pg. 113
- yellow pepper bruschetta, pg. 115

MAKES 1 LOAF

There is no doubt that this page will be frequently referenced. Keep a bookmark handy.

basic rice

Bring water to a boil in a large saucepan. When boiling, add rice, salt and butter. Reduce heat to low and allow rice to simmer 20 minutes, or until liquid is absorbed. Remove from heat and fluff with a fork. If all water has not been absorbed, cover and allow to stand for 5 additional minutes.

$4^{1}/_{4}$ cups water
2 cups rice
1 teaspoon salt
2 tablespoons butter

see:
- red beans and rice, pg. 60
- grilled tuna roll-ups, pg. 75
- grilled vegetable and sun-dried tomato paste wraps, pg. 78
- shredded beef wraps, pg. 90
- chicken wraps with a whole lot of citrus, pg. 91
- pork fried rice, pg. 117
- rice pudding, pg. 118

MAKES 3 CUPS

asparagus

Simmer water in a shallow pan. Cut woody ends from asparagus. Place spears in water. Simmer for about 3 minutes, or just until tender. Do not overcook. When tender, remove from water.

MAKES 8 SERVINGS

½ cup water
4 lb. asparagus

see:

- an asparagus frittata tonight, pg. 107
- sesame asparagus salad, pg. 114
- spring asparagus gratin, pg. 130

corn

Bring water to a boil in a large stockpot. Place corn in water. Simmer for about 4 minutes, or just until tender. Do not overcook. When tender, remove from water.

MAKES 8 SERVINGS

½ gallon water
12 ears fresh corn, shucked

see:

- a little hot corn chowder, pg. 120
- sweet corn and sugar pea salad, pg. 121

Two shades of yellow – the tumeric and peppers give this sauce its color. Heavy cream washes it into one smooth sauce.

mellow yellow sauce

In a skillet, sauté onion, garlic and peppers until onion is translucent and peppers are crisp-tender. Add heavy cream and bring to a rapid boil. Reduce heat to low and simmer. Add chicken stock and season with tumeric, salt and pepper.

1 large onion, diced
2 cloves garlic, minced
4 yellow peppers, seeded and diced
$1/4$ cup heavy cream
2 cups chicken stock
dash tumeric
salt and pepper to taste

see:
• yellow chicken, pg. 50

MAKES 8 SERVINGS

for the weekend

It is not unusual for criticism to fly around the dinner table when roast beef is the subject. Harsh words like "the meat's too tough" or "it's dry" are not unfamiliar to the home chef. This sirloin rarely disappoints – the meat is tender and succulent.

roast beef

Heat oven to 500°. Place beef in a shallow roasting pan and place in oven. Roast for 15 minutes. Reduce heat to 350° and roast for another 1½ hours, or until a meat thermometer inserted in thickest part of the roast reads 140°, or medium. Remove from oven. Let stand for 10 minutes; cut into thin slices and serve with pan juices.

1 sirloin roast, 6 lb.

see:

• brimming with beef quesadillas, pg. 85

• why is it Sicilian pasta? pg. 89

• shredded beef wraps, pg. 90

MAKES 8-10 SERVINGS

Montreal shares the French and Canadian cultures.
This pork borrows a little of each –
a marriage of cooking heritages.

Montreal pork roast

In a bowl, whisk maple syrup, pineapple juice, brown sugar, soy sauce, garlic and herbs. Place pork roast in a baking pan. Pour half the marinade over meat and refrigerate remainder. Cover and refrigerate roast for at least 8 hours. Baste periodically. Heat oven to 375°. Remove roast from pan and discard marinade. Place pork in roasting pan. Roast for about 1½ hours. Pour remaining marinade over roast and return to oven. Roast for another 30 minutes or until juices run clear. Transfer roast to a serving platter. Juices may be strained and used as gravy.

1 cup maple syrup
1 cup pineapple juice
¼ cup brown sugar, packed
¼ cup soy sauce
6 cloves garlic, minced
2 tablespoons chopped
   fresh rosemary
2 tablespoons chopped fresh thyme
2 tablespoons chopped fresh parsley
5-6 lb. boneless pork loin

see:
• pork fried rice, page 117

MAKES 6-8 SERVINGS

Pork tenderloin is the Rolls Royce of the pork family — tender and meaty.

pork tenderloin

Heat oven to 350°. Place 2 tenderloins in a baking pan and 2 tenderloins in another. Spoon plum sauce over one pair. Place garlic cloves over other 2 tenderloins. Roast for 1 1/2 hours, or until meat is white when cut.

Reserve 2 tenderloins for weekday meals; serve the plum sauce for Chinese dishes.

tenderloin with mushrooms

In a saute pan, fry the mushrooms slowly until tender. Pour stock into tenderloin roasting pan and gently stir to incorporate cooking juices. Add flour and water to an airtight container, and shake well to blend. Pour mixture into roasting pan. Add sherry. Add mushrooms. Simmer until thickened. Salt and pepper to taste. Reserve half the sauce to be used during the week. Slice tenderloins. Arrange slices on individual plates and spoon sauce over sliced pork.

4 pork tenderloins
* 1/2 cup plum sauce, pg. 24
8 cloves garlic
1/2 cup mushrooms
2 cups chicken stock
4 tablespoons flour
1/2 cup water
1/4 cup sherry
salt and pepper to taste

see:
- a pork tenderloin both sweet and sour, pg. 81

MAKES 4-8 SERVINGS

Most supermarkets carry 12 oz. tubes of bulk sausage. Flatter your butcher and you'll probably walk away with something much leaner and tasty.

naked sausage

Brown sausage in a large skillet. Discard excess fat. Divide cooked sausage into 2 equal portions. Refrigerate in airtight containers.

2 lb. bulk sausage

see:

- homestead sausage and apples, pg. 41

- cowboy sausage and gravy, pg. 82

- a casserole made with sausage, pg. 83

MAKES 6-10 SERVINGS

A meal for a cowboy or girl – round up large apples and stuff them full of the sausage mixture; serve them next to potatoes or hot buttered noodles.

homestead sausage and apples

Heat oven to 350°. Wash and core apples. In a sauté pan, sauté onion until translucent. Add garlic and sauté briefly. In a large bowl, combine sausage and onion mixture. Spoon sausage mixture into apples. Place in a baking dish. Spoon brown sugar over top of each apple. Fill baking dish with about 1 inch of water and place in oven. Bake for 45 minutes, or until apples are tender. Remove from oven and cool slightly before serving.

8 large Rome apples
1 medium onion, minced
1 clove garlic, minced
* 1 lb. cooked sausage, pg. 40
¼ cup brown sugar

MAKES 8 SERVINGS

use:

• naked sausage, pg. 40

Grill these over hot, hot coals to sear that
sweet honey-mustard flavor deep into the
heart of the steaks.

honey-mustard steaks

Place steaks on a grill over hot coals or under a broiler and brush with honey mustard. Grill or broil for about 15 minutes, or until cooked to your desire. Turn once and baste. Remove from grill or broiler. Sprinkle with cayenne pepper and season with salt and pepper. Serve immediately.

3 boneless sirloin steaks, $^3/_4$ lb. each
* $^1/_4$ cup honey mustard, pg. 19
dash cayenne pepper
salt and pepper to taste

see:
- honey mustard, pg. 19
- brimming with beef quesadillas, pg. 85
- Caesar steak salad, pg. 88
- steak and citrus salsa crepes, pg. 151

MAKES 6 SERVINGS

Anyone can buy corned beef at the store, but not everyone is daring enough to make it. Double the recipe if you plan on using corned beef as a weekday meal. Remember that the meat will not be pink because nitrates were not used in the corning process.

corned beef

Rinse meat. Heat water in a large pot. Add salt and stir to dissolve. Add brisket, 5 peppercorns, 2 mashed garlic cloves and 2 teaspoons pickling spice. Use a small plate or bowl to weigh meat down inside pot. Cover and refrigerate for 48 hours. After 2 days, remove meat from brine. Rinse meat well and discard brine. Place meat back in pot. Add fresh water to cover. Add 5 peppercorns, 2 teaspoons pickling spice and 2 mashed garlic cloves. Simmer partially covered for about 4 hours.

4-5 lb. lean beef brisket
4 quarts hot water
1½ lb. salt
10 peppercorns
4 cloves garlic, mashed
4 teaspoons pickling spice

see:

• a quiche of corned beef, pg. 86

• red flannel hash, pg. 87

MAKES 6-8 SERVINGS

The anticipated syrup shellacs this ham.
Prime it first with a good, strong coat, and then tidy up your paint job, patching any open holes with leftover glaze.
Your handiwork is bound to be appreciated.

honey-mustard glazed ham

Heat oven to 325°. Cut diagonal slices in ham and place in roasting pan. Brush with honey-mustard. Bake for about 1½ hours, basting with honey-mustard juices periodically. Remove from oven and allow ham to rest for several minutes. Transfer to a serving platter.

1 ready-to-eat ham, skin removed, excess fat trimmed
* ¼ - ½ cup honey mustard, pg. 19

see:
- lightning paella, pg. 68
- ham and bread, pg. 84
- creole ham casserole, pg. 98
- pink loaf, pg. 99
- white bean soup, pg. 119
- carrots Marrakesh, pg. 133
- ham and Gorgonzola crepes, pg. 150

MAKES 6-8 SERVINGS

The vinegar tenderizes the chicken, the honey adds
a syrupy quality and the mustard gives it tang.

honey-mustard chicken

Pat chicken dry and dredge in flour. Heat oil in a large sauté pan. Place chicken in hot oil and sauté until lightly brown. Add honey mustard thinned with a few tablespoons of water. Simmer until liquid reduces. Serve chicken immediately with honey-mustard sauce spooned on top.

4 boneless chicken breast halves
flour for dredging
2 tablespoons canola oil
* $1/2$ cup honey mustard, pg. 19
water for thinning mustard

use:
• honey mustard, pg. 19

MAKES 4 SERVINGS

The added walnuts give this dish an interesting
texture and surprising nuttiness.

sweet onion chicken

Finely grind walnuts with a blender or food processor. Add flour and mix just until incorporated. In a small bowl, beat egg and water. Heat oil in a large sauté pan. With a mallet, pound chicken between two sheets of waxed paper. Dip in egg wash and flour mixture. Finish dredging all chicken breasts and sauté until golden brown on both sides. Remove chicken. Drain excess oil from pan and pour onion sauce into pan to heat. Place chicken breasts on individual plates, season with salt and pepper and spoon sauce over each serving.

$1/4$ cup walnuts
$1/4$ cup flour
1 egg
$1/4$ cup water
3 tablespoons canola oil
4 boneless chicken breast halves
flour for dredging
* 1 cup sweet onion sauce, pg. 20
salt and pepper to taste

use:
• sweet onion sauce, pg. 20

MAKES 4 SERVINGS

This chicken dish defines the word "café." It is casual and chic at the same time. And here's a bonus: it requires little preparation.

café chicken

Heat oven to 350°. Pat chicken breasts dry and dredge in flour. Heat oil in a large sauté pan. Lightly sauté each chicken breast and place in a large baking dish. Pour orange juice, kumquats and brown sugar over breasts. Bake for about 1 1/2 hours or until juices run clear. Set aside 6 breast halves for weekday use, removing meat from bones. With the remaining 4, place each breast half on an individual plate and spoon thickened juice and fruit over chicken.

10 chicken breast halves
flour for dredging
1/4 cup canola oil
2 cups orange juice
1 can (6.5 oz.) kumquats
1/2 cup brown sugar, packed

see:
- pockets of chicken, pg. 105
- down at the café ranchero salad, pg. 106

MAKES 4 SERVINGS

This is a wonderfully utilitarian recipe and the addition of tomatoes makes the meat melt-in-your-mouth tender.

chicken in a pot

Rinse chicken. Place all ingredients in a large stockpot. Simmer for about 3 hours, skimming fat periodically. There are two choices of how to proceed after removing the chicken from the pot. You may serve the soup unstrained in a large bowl with the vegetables and chicken meat immediately. Or you may strain the stock, reserving the vegetables for other uses. The stock may be used as a soup and sauce base. If frozen, it will keep well for up to 3 months. Pour some stock into plastic quart containers. Transfer some stock to ice cube trays and freeze. After stock cubes are solid, transfer them to a plastic freezer bag. These may be used when only a small amount of stock is needed. Remove chicken from bones and reserve for other meals.

1 roasting chicken, 4 lb.
3 quarts water
2 large onions, quartered
4 carrots, peeled and cut into
    sections
3 stalks celery, sliced
3 medium tomatoes, cut into quarters
2 parsnips, sliced
6 sprigs fresh parsley
salt and pepper to taste

see:
- chicken egg rolls, pg. 51
- mushroom and caramelized
    onion sauce, pg. 56
- real McCoy risotto, pg. 62
- lightning paella, pg. 68
- creamy chicken salad, pg. 84
- Gruyère crepes, pg. 152
- bread soup, pg. 110

MAKES 4 SERVINGS

As long as the oven is on, cooking two chickens
is a savings in time and energy.

roasted chicken

Heat oven to 350°. Rinse chickens and place in a large roasting pan. Place garlic inside one chicken cavity and lemons inside second chicken. Roast until juices run clear, about 1½ to 2 hours. Reserve lemon chicken for weekday meals. Use garlic chicken immediately. Squeeze flesh from garlic cloves and add to mashed potatoes.

2 roasting chickens, 3½ lb. each
1 bulb garlic
2 whole lemons, skin pricked with fork

see:
- Gruyère crepes, pg. 152
- chicken wraps with a whole
  lot of citrus, pg. 91
- chicken stew with garbanzos, pg. 92
- Far East salad, pg. 93
- creamy chicken salad, pg. 94
- tomato chicken penne, pg. 95
- chicken picatta, pg. 96
- honey-mustard chicken pitas, pg. 97
- look at the colorful salad, pg. 108

MAKES 4 SERVINGS

A little spicy, a little Indian, this is a recipe
that will appeal to anyone's palate.

yellow chicken

In a small bowl, combine yogurt, lime juice, curry paste, ginger and garlic. Blend well. Dip each chicken breast in yogurt mixture, covering completely. Place chicken in a baking pan, cover with plastic wrap and refrigerate for at least 1 hour. Heat oil in a heavy skillet until hot. Add chicken and sauté on both sides until completely cooked. In a small saucepan over low heat, heat yellow pepper sauce. Add salt, pepper and cayenne to taste. Remove chicken breasts from pan and place on plates. Pour yellow pepper sauce next to chicken. Garnish with fresh mint. Serve immediately.

2 tablespoons nonfat yogurt
2 tablespoons fresh lime juice
2 teaspoons mild curry paste
1 teaspoon grated fresh ginger
1 teaspoon crushed fresh garlic
4 boneless chicken breast halves
2 tablespoons canola oil
* 1 cup mellow yellow sauce, pg. 34
fresh mint for garnish
salt and pepper to taste
dash cayenne pepper

MAKES 4 SERVINGS

see:
• mellow yellow sauce, pg. 34

Popular as an appetizer, egg rolls make a handsome side dish or snack. Keep them in the freezer for unexpected guests.

chicken egg rolls

Combine chicken, water chestnuts, bamboo shoots, bean sprouts, cabbage, green onions, mushrooms, garlic, ginger, sugar, sesame oil and soy sauce in a large bowl. Stir to combine. Cover and marinate for 30 minutes.

Working with one egg roll wrapper at a time, spoon about 2 tablespoons of filling on one corner of wrapper. Fold corner over filling. Fold each side in. Brush beaten egg on inside surface. Roll and press to seal. Continue until all wrappers are filled. In a deep fat fryer, heat oil to 375°. Fry egg rolls until golden brown and crisp. Remove and drain on paper towels. Serve immediately or cool completely, place in freezer bags and freeze. Serve with plum sauce.

* 1 cup diced cooked chicken, pg. 47
1/4 cup chopped water chestnuts
1/4 cup chopped bamboo shoots
1 cup bean sprouts
1 cup shredded green or Chinese cabbage
2 green onions, chopped
1/2 cup chopped shiitake mushrooms
1 clove garlic, minced
1 teaspoon minced fresh ginger
1/2 teaspoon sugar
1 tablespoon sesame oil
2 tablespoons soy sauce
1 pkg. (16 oz.) egg roll wrappers
1 egg, beaten
canola oil for frying
* plum sauce, pg. 24

see:
• chicken in a pot, pg. 47
• plum sauce, pg. 24

MAKES 4 SERVINGS

Ground turkey has quickly gained a reputation
as the new "All-American" hamburger.

turkey burgers

Toast bread and use a food processor to make breadcrumbs. Reserve $^1/_3$. Transfer the rest to a temporary container. Cut onions into quarters and process in the food processor workbowl until minced. Add turkey, $^1/_2$ cup mushrooms, garlic, breadcrumbs from the temporary container and parsley to food processor. Add cayenne, salt and pepper. Process until incorporated. Transfer half to an airtight container and refrigerate. Make patties from remaining turkey mixture. Dip patties in reserved breadcrumbs. Heat oil in a large sauté pan. Brown patties on both sides until golden. Remove from pan and add remaining mushrooms. Add 1 cup of the chicken broth. In a small bowl, combine flour with a few spoonfuls of remaining chicken broth. Add to pan and stir gently over low heat to thicken. Add remaining chicken broth and sherry. Cook until thickened, stirring periodically. Transfer patties to individual plates and spoon sauce over patties.

6 slices white bread
2 small onions
2 lb. ground turkey
$^1/_2$ cup sliced mushrooms
2 cloves garlic
1 tablespoon chopped fresh flat-leaf
  parsley
dash cayenne pepper
salt and pepper to taste
canola oil for frying
$^1/_2$ lb. mushrooms, sliced
2 cups chicken broth
$^1/_4$ cup flour
2 tablespoons sherry, optional

see:
- unstuffed cabbage, pg. 100
- turkey meatballs, pg. 102

MAKES 3 SERVINGS

Sweet potatoes complement many main courses but are especially good with a pork or beef roast.

sweet potatoes and apples

Heat oven to 350°. Butter a baking dish. Slice potatoes and arrange a layer on the bottom of baking dish. Alternate layers of apples and potatoes. Top with sugar, molasses, spices and remaining butter. Drizzle with lemon juice. Add apple juice. Bake until cooked down and tender, about 45 minutes to 1 hour. Serve as a side dish.

6 sweet potatoes, baked or boiled
2 cups sliced apples
$1/2$ cup brown sugar, packed
2 tablespoons molasses
$1/2$ teaspoon nutmeg
$1/2$ teaspoon cinnamon
$1/4$ cup butter
1 teaspoon lemon juice
$1/2$ cup apple juice

MAKES 4 SERVINGS

Having cooked eggplant in the refrigerator is a real time-saver. You might serve this with a crusty bread and a hearty bowl of soup.

eggplant casserole

Heat oven to 375°. Grease a baking dish and set aside. In a large bowl, combine eggplant, onion, garlic, spices, milk and eggs. In a small bowl, combine breadcrumbs and olive oil. Stir well. In baking dish, alternate layers of eggplant mixture with layers of breadcrumbs. End with a layer of breadcrumbs. Top with mozzarella. Bake for about 30 minutes or until the cheese is bubbly.

* flesh from 1 roasted eggplant, pg. 27
1 onion, minced
1 clove garlic, minced
salt and pepper to taste
dash cayenne pepper
$1/2$ cup milk
2 eggs, beaten
$1/2$ cup breadcrumbs
2 tablespoons olive oil
1 cup shredded mozzarella cheese

use:
• roasted eggplant, pg. 27

MAKES 4 SERVINGS

You can't really live a full life without a recipe for smashed potatoes. Make these with whole milk, half-and-half or cream. Lightweights take note: chicken broth is an acceptable substitute.

smashed potatoes

In a bowl, beat potatoes and butter until smooth. Add milk a little at a time and season with salt and pepper. Beat until fluffy, adding more liquid if necessary. Serve immediately.

* 2 lb. cooked potatoes, pg. 27
3 tablespoons butter
1/3 cup milk, cream or chicken broth, warmed slightly
salt and pepper to taste

see:

- cooked potatoes, pg. 27
- farmhouse potato cakes, pg. 124
- apple mash, pg. 126
- tomato-pesto gnocchi, pg. 128
- cowboy sausage and gravy, pg. 82
- a quiche of corned beef, pg. 86

MAKES 4 SERVINGS

Wait. This can't be French onion soup – there is no Gruyère cheese. But the onions are caramelized the same way – reminds me of that little Paris Bistro we ate in back in the autumn of '67. Remember?

mushroom and caramelized onion soup

In a medium stockpot, heat oil and add onion. Sauté onion until translucent. Add mushrooms and continue to cook slowly. Onions should caramelize slightly. Add chicken or beef stock and parsley. Simmer for about 20 minutes. Add lemon juice and simmer for another 10 minutes. Adjust seasonings. Reserve half for chicken picatta, page 96.

¹/₄ cup olive oil
1 large onion, minced
2 pkg. (10 oz. each) button mushrooms, sliced
* 6 cups chicken or beef broth, pg. 48
2 tablespoons minced fresh flat-leaf
   parsley
juice of 1 lemon
salt and pepper to taste

see:
• chicken in a pot, pg. 48
• chicken picatta, pg. 96

MAKES 4 SERVINGS

The days of wine and roses might be appropriate background music while you cook.

wine and rosemary shrimp

Peel and devein shrimp. Heat oil in large sauté pan. Add shallots, shrimp and garlic. Sauté shrimp until pink. Add lemon juice, rosemary and white wine. Simmer until juices have reduced slightly. Remove from heat and transfer shrimp to individual plates. Spoon sauce over shrimp, season with salt and pepper and serve.

4 lb. raw shrimp
1/4 cup olive oil
2 shallots, minced
2 cloves garlic, minced
1/2 cup lemon juice
1 tablespoon minced fresh rosemary
1/4 cup white wine
salt and pepper to taste

see:

- composed salad of shrimp and apple, pg. 111
- baked shrimp, pg. 112
- lightning paella, pg. 68

MAKES 4 SERVINGS

storing your foodstuffs

a word about storage:

Heavyweight freezer bags are excellent for storing food, but nothing keeps indefinitely. Do not plan on keeping anything for more than three months, as the taste and texture will dissipate in the freezer. Plastic containers are good for storing cooked foods. Don't try to freeze anything with milk in it – creamy soups for example – the milk will separate.

When storing, make sure the container or bag is airtight. Since most freezers are now of the frost-free variety, if there is an opening in your container, the freezer will suck all the moisture out of your food.

Most foods you make won't keep for an entire week in the refrigerator, so do be careful to remember when you slid that container toward the back. Mayonnaise, salsa and mustard keep longer because they contain acid which acts as something of a preservative.

A little lemon goes a long way. Just the right amount of acid is enough for this fleshy fish to continue its run – into your mouth.

lemon-crusted salmon steaks

Heat broiler. In a large bowl, combine breadcrumbs, parsley, chives, lemon zest, salt and pepper. Transfer mixture to a pie pan or a flat surface covered with waxed paper. Brush steaks with olive oil and place under broiler for about 4 minutes, or until just cooked. Remove salmon from broiler and dredge in breadcrumb mixture. Return salmon to broiler and continue cooking until done and crust is golden brown.

$1/2$ cup dry breadcrumbs
1 tablespoon minced fresh flat-leaf parsley
1 tablespoon minced fresh chives
2 teaspoons chopped lemon zest
8 salmon steaks, 4 oz. each
2 tablespoons olive oil

MAKES 4 SERVINGS

see:
• salmon pasta salad, pg. 77

This is a tradition coming out of Louisiana. It stores well in the refrigerator and can be reheated quickly.

red beans and rice

Fry bacon in a large skillet. When crisp, remove bacon from skillet and add butter, onion, garlic and celery. Sauté until tender. Add tomatoes and seasoning. Add beans and simmer until beans are very tender, about 30 minutes. Serve over cooked rice.

4 strips bacon
3 tablespoons butter
1 yellow onion, diced
4 cloves garlic, sliced
3 stalks celery, diced
2 cups crushed, peeled tomatoes
2 tablespoons Creole seasoning
salt and pepper to taste
4 cups red beans, cooked
* 2 cups cooked rice, page 32

see:
• basic rice, pg. 32
• stuffed acorn squash, pg. 69

MAKES 4 SERVINGS

As duck has increased in popularity, more supermarkets are willing to stock the bird year 'round. This glaze aids in producing a tender and lustrous bird.

glazed duck

Heat oven to 400°. Rinse ducks and place breast side up in a large roasting pan. Place in oven and roast for 30 minutes. Remove from oven and reduce heat to 350°. Baste ducks with plum sauce and return ducks to oven. Continue roasting for about 1 hour, basting every 15 minutes until ducks are completely cooked. Remove from oven. Transfer ducks to a serving platter. Let ducks stand for about 10 minutes before carving. Reserve 1 duck for a weekday meal.

2 ducklings, 5 lb. each
* 2 cups plum sauce, pg. 24

see:

• plum sauce, pg. 24

• moo shu duck, pg. 72

• duck quesadillas, pg. 73

MAKES 4 SERVINGS

Unlike the familiar white steamed rice, risotto cooks
up a bit on the soupy side when perfectly prepared.
As it stands, it continues to soak up liquid.

real McCoy risotto

In a large saucepan, sauté onion in oil over medium heat until lightly brown. Add rice and sauté for about 2 minutes. Add wine and simmer until evaporated. Add enough stock to cover rice. Stir for about 8 minutes, or until liquid has absorbed. Keep adding liquid in intervals until absorbed and all liquid is used. It should take about 20 minutes for rice to become tender and all liquid to be absorbed. Remove from heat and season with salt and pepper. Add butter and cheese. Serve immediately, reserving half.

2 medium yellow onions, diced
6 tablespoons olive oil
4 cups Arborio rice
1 cup white wine
6 cups chicken stock
salt and pepper to taste
$1/4$ cup butter
1 cup grated Parmesan cheese

see:
• risotto cakes, pg. 76

MAKES 8 SERVINGS

Start the marinade in the morning, and by dinnertime the tuna will have had a chance to soak up the flavors of the marinade.

tuna with citrus salsa

Place 4 tuna fillets in a large glass baking ban. Pour salsa over fillets and cover with plastic wrap. Marinate in the refrigerator for several hours. Heat broiler. Broil all 8 tuna fillets for about 4 minutes on each side, or until cooked through. Cut 4 marinated fillets into slices on the diagonal and serve. Reserve 4 unmarinated cooked steaks for the week.

8 ahi tuna fillets, 4 oz. each
* 1 cup citrus salsa, pg. 23

see:

• citrus salsa, pg 23

• salad nicoise, pg. 70

• grilled tuna roll-ups, pg. 75

MAKES 4 SERVINGS

Cooked on an indoor or outdoor grill, these vegetables
can make an entire meal or a side dish.

grilled vegetables

Prepare a medium-hot grill. In a large bowl, combine oil, herbs, garlic and salt. Cover and set aside for at least 30 minutes. When grill is hot, baste vegetables with oil mixture and grill until tender. Reserve half for another meal.

1 cup olive oil

1 tablespoon chopped fresh basil

1 tablespoon chopped fresh flat-leaf parsley

1 teaspoon minced garlic

$1/2$ teaspoon salt

4-6 Italian or Japanese eggplants, cut in half

1 leek, cut into quarters

3 zucchini, cut into quarters

1 Vidalia or Walla Walla onion, thinly sliced

1 tomato, cut into quarters

8 large mushrooms

see:

• grilled vegetable foccacia, pg. 71

• grilled vegetable and sun-dried tomato pesto wraps, pg. 78

MAKES 8 SERVINGS

This hearty soup has its heritage in the Carribean, but has become a favorite in other cooking realms, specifically Southwestern cooking and Latin American cuisine.

black bean soup

In a large stockpot, melt butter and lightly sauté onion and celery until translucent. Add beans and remaining ingredients. Cover and simmer over low heat for 45 minutes, or until beans are tender, but not mushy. Using a wooden spoon, mash enough beans against the side of pot to thicken liquid. Remove bay leaf and add cayenne pepper. Season with salt and pepper. Serve in deep soup bowls or serve over rice.

2 tablespoons butter
1 cup chopped yellow onion
$1/4$ cup diced celery
4 cups black beans, cooked
3 cups chicken stock
$1^1/2$ cups diced ham
1 bay leaf
$1/2$ teaspoon dried oregano
$1/2$ cup chopped red bell pepper
$1/2$ cup chopped green bell pepper
dash cayenne pepper
salt and pepper to taste
lemon slices for garnish

see:
• Cuban black beans and shrimp "chili," pg. 74
• Cuban chicken, pg. 79

MAKES 4 SERVINGS

plates for the week

This quick paella is nearly as fast as lightning.
Just what you want out of a meal.

lightning paella

In a large saucepan over medium-high heat, add shrimp, butter, broth, peas, seasoning and rice. Bring to a boil. Stir in ham, olives, lemon juice and tomatoes. Cover and remove from heat. Let stand for 5 minutes. With a fork, stir in salt, pepper and cilantro. Serve immediately.

* 1 cup cooked shrimp, pg. 57
2 tablespoons butter
1$^1/_2$ cups chicken broth
1 cup green peas
2 tablespoons Creole Seasoning
1$^1/_2$ cups quick-cooking rice
* $^1/_2$ cup cubed cooked ham, pg. 44
$^1/_2$ cup black olives
2 tablespoons lemon juice
1 cup cherry tomatoes
salt and pepper to taste
1 tablespoon minced fresh cilantro

use:
- honey-mustard glazed ham, pg. 44
- wine and rosemary shrimp, pg. 57

MAKES 4 SERVINGS

Acorn squash is most readily available in the autumn and winter months. Choose those squash that are heavy and dark green. Beware of the speckled squash, as this is an indication of a bad squash.

stuffed acorn squash

Heat oven to 375°. Cut squash in half; scoop out strings and seeds and discard. Place squash flat side down in a baking dish. Add $1/2$-inch water to dish. Bake for 45 minutes, or until edges of squash are brown and flesh is tender when pricked with a fork. Remove from oven and turn squash over. Fill each empty cavity with red beans and rice. Return to oven and bake until squash has completely cooked. Remove from oven and serve immediately.

2 large acorn squash
* 2 cups red beans and rice, pg. 60

MAKES 4 SERVINGS

use:
• red beans and rice, pg. 60

Images of French Provence may come to mind with this salad.
A crisp white wine is all this salad requires.

salad nicoise

Peel garlic clove and rub clove over the bottom of salad bowl. Add greens, tomatoes, cucumber, eggs, olives, tuna and anchovies to bowl. In a small bowl, whisk salt, pepper, oil, vinegar and sugar. Drizzle over top and toss salad to combine.

1 clove garlic, chopped
1 pkg.(1 lb.) or 4 cups mixed greens
2 ripe tomatoes, cut into bite-sized
   pieces
1 cucumber, peeled, seeded and
   cubed
2 hard-boiled eggs, chopped
$1/2$ cup nicoise olives
* 1 cup flaked, cooked tuna, pg. 63
4 anchovies, chopped
salt and pepper to taste
$1/2$ cup olive oil
$1/4$ cup red wine vinegar
1 teaspoon sugar

use:
• tuna with citrus salsa, pg. 63

MAKES 4 SERVINGS

If your local grocer doesn't carry focaccia bread, shame on him. But don't give him too hard a time: day-old sourdough or another specialty bread can hold the batch of vegetables equally well.

grilled vegetable focaccia

Heat broiler. Place focaccia on a baking sheet. Lightly oil top of focaccia. Spoon vegetables over top. Cover with cheese and pepper. Place under broiler until cheese has melted. Serve immediately.

four 8-inch round pieces of focaccia
1 tablespoon olive oil
* ½ portion grilled vegetables, pg. 64
1 cup grated fontina cheese
pepper to taste

MAKES 4 SERVINGS

use:

• grilled vegetables, pg. 64

Mandarin pancakes are easily found at the supermarket or at your local Asian grocery; however, you can just as easily use crepes (see page 18).

moo shu duck

Heat oil in large skillet or wok. Stir-fry mushrooms, bamboo shoots, water chestnuts, Chinese cabbage and green onions. Add soy sauce, sugar and ginger. Add duck. Stir to blend. When duck is thoroughly warmed, remove from heat. Spoon duck mixture on center of each pancake. Spoon a bit of plum sauce over filling. Fold each side in to seal. Serve immediately.

$1/2$ cup vegetable oil
$1/2$ cup chopped white mushrooms
$1/2$ cup bamboo shoots
$1/4$ cup diced water chestnuts
$1/2$ cup shredded Chinese cabbage
2 green onions, chopped
2 tablespoons soy sauce
2 teaspoons sugar
pinch ground ginger
* 2 cups shredded cooked duck
   meat, pg. 61
* 8 Mandarin pancakes or crepes,
   pg. 18
* $1/2$ cup plum sauce, pg. 24

use:

• crepes, pg. 18

• plum sauce, pg. 24

• glazed duck, pg. 61

MAKES 4 SERVINGS

Using duck rather than chicken turns a commoners' dish into a gourmet offering. Adjust the heat of the spice and peppers to your own taste.

duck quesadillas

In a large skillet over medium heat, heat 1 tablespoon of the oil and add onion and jalapeño peppers. When onions are translucent, add chili powder, cumin and cilantro. Stir to blend. Add duck and cook until heated through. Transfer to a bowl. Add remaining 1 tablespoon oil to skillet over low heat. Lay tortilla flat in skillet, add duck mixture and cheese and cook until cheese melts. Fold quesadilla in half and serve with salsa and sour cream.

2 tablespoons vegetable oil
1 yellow onion, diced
1-2 jalapeño peppers, minced
1-2 teaspoons chili powder
$1/4$ teaspoon ground cumin
1 tablespoon minced fresh cilantro
* 1 cup cooked diced duck meat,
   pg. 61
1 cup shredded Monterey Jack cheese
eight 8-inch tortillas
* salsa, pg. 22 or pg. 23
sour cream

use:
• glazed duck, pg. 61
• tomato salsa, pg. 22 or
• sunny citrus salsa, pg. 23

MAKES 4 SERVINGS

Is it a soup or is it a chili? This certainly has elements of both. But to save you from agonizing over it, we've called it a chili.

Cuban black beans and shrimp "chili"

In a large skillet over medium-high heat, heat oil. Sauté onion, bell pepper and garlic until onion is transclucent and bell peppers are tender. Add beans, shrimp and spices. Simmer, covered, until beans are heated through, about 10 minutes. Add lemon juice and season with salt and pepper. Serve in deep soup bowls.

2 tablespoons olive oil
1 yellow onion, chopped
1 green bell pepper, seeded and diced
2 cloves garlic, minced
* 4 cups black beans, pg. 65
2 cups small shrimp, deveined and cleaned
1 teaspoon dried oregano
$1/2$ teaspoon dried thyme
1 teaspoon lemon juice
salt and pepper to taste

use:
• black bean soup, pg. 65

MAKES 4 SERVINGS

What's the difference between fusion, Asian and Japanese cuisine? That is something you might want to ponder as you stuff your face with this roll-up. Components of each, maybe.

grilled tuna roll-ups

Cut tuna fillets into strips. Layer tuna, rice, chestnuts and green onions on tortillas. Sprinkle with sesame seeds and brush with plum sauce. Roll up tortillas and eat out of hand.

* 4 grilled tuna fillets, 4 oz. each, pg. 63
* 1 cup cooked white rice, pg. 32
$1/4$ cup sliced water chestnuts
2 tablespoons chopped green onions
four 10-inch tortillas
2 tablespoons sesame seeds
* 2 tablespoons plum sauce, pg. 24

use:

• plum sauce, pg. 24

• basic rice, pg. 32

• tuna with citrus salsa, pg. 63

MAKES 4 SERVINGS

Risotto: an old Italian peasant dish that is somewhat time-consuming. The stirring has already been done. Now you just need volunteers for the eating.

risotto cakes

Butter a 9-x-13-inch baking dish. In a large bowl, beat eggs just until foamy. Add risotto and parsley. Stir to blend. Transfer risotto mixture to baking dish and spread evenly. Cover and refrigerate until very firm. Cut risotto into even squares and gently mold into rounds about $1/2$-inch thick. Lightly flour each cake and place on a baking sheet. Refrigerate until firm. Over medium-high heat, heat a skillet and add oil. Sauté risotto cakes until golden brown on both sides. Drain on paper towels. Serve immediately.

1 tablespoon butter
1 egg
* $1/2$ portion risotto, pg. 62
1 tablespoon chopped fresh flat-leaf parsley
$1/2$ cup flour
2 tablespoons olive oil

use:
• real McCoy risotto, pg. 62

MAKES 4 SERVINGS

It's that heart-wrenching decision again: which pasta shape to use? Here's a bit of advice: a smaller shape doesn't interfere with the larger chunks of salmon.

salmon pasta salad

Cook pasta in boiling water until tender; drain. Add oil to pasta and toss to coat. Let pasta cool; transfer to large bowl. Add salmon, green onions and lemon zest. In a small bowl, whisk to combine basil, lemon juice, sugar, salt and pepper. Pour dressing over pasta salad and toss to combine.

* 8 oz. fresh pasta, pg. 16
1 tablespoon olive oil
* 2 cups cubed cooked salmon, pg. 59
1/2 cup chopped green onions
1 tablespoon chopped fresh basil
2 tablespoons freshly squeezed lemon juice
zest of 1 lemon, minced
1/2 teaspoon sugar
salt and pepper to taste

use:
• pasta dough, pg. 16
• lemon-crusted salmon steaks, pg. 59

MAKES 4 SERVINGS

This combines the sharpness of Gorgonzola with mild vegetables for a balance of flavors. If you prefer an even sharper taste, try radish sprouts, rather than bean sprouts.

grilled vegetable and sun-dried tomato pesto wraps

In a large bowl, combine vegetables and pesto. Lay vegetables, rice, cheese and sprouts in center of tortillas. Fold tortilla sides in and ends up to seal. Cut in half or on the diagonal. Serve and eat out of hand.

* $1/2$ portion grilled vegetables, diced, pg. 64
* 2 cups cooked rice, pg. 32
* $1/2$ cup tomato pesto, pg. 21
1 cup crumbled Gorgonzola cheese
$1/2$ cup bean sprouts
four 10-inch tortillas

use:

• tomato pesto, pg. 21

• basic rice, pg. 32

• grilled vegetables, pg. 64

MAKES 4 SERVINGS

The spices here are pure Caribbean.

Cuban chicken

In a large skillet over medium-high heat, heat oil and sauté chicken lightly on both sides. Add onion, green pepper, carrot, celery, jalapeño pepper and garlic. Sauté vegetables until onion is translucent. Add tomatoes, lemon juice, beans, cumin and cilantro. Reduce heat, cover and simmer for 30 minutes. Remove cover and continue to cook for about 10 minutes until liquid reduces. Serve immediately.

2 tablespoons olive oil
4 chicken breast halves
1 yellow onion, diced
1 green bell pepper, seeded and diced
1 carrot, peeled and diced
1 stalk celery, diced
1 jalapeño pepper, minced
1 clove garlic, minced
1 cup peeled, diced tomatoes
1 tablespoon lemon juice
* 2 cups black beans, pg. 65
1 teaspoon ground cumin
1 tablespoon minced fresh cilantro

use:
• black bean soup, pg. 65

MAKES 4 SERVINGS

Pull together this gourmet offering in less than an hour; nary a soul will conceive it was possible.

sweet onion pork chops

Dredge pork chops in flour. Place between sheets of waxed paper and pound with a food mallet until chops are half the original thickness. Heat oil in a sauté pan. Transfer pork chops to pan and sauté until lightly brown on both sides. Pour sweet onion sauce over pork chops. Cover and simmer for about 20 minutes. Remove from heat and place chops on individual plates. Spoon sauce over chops. Sauce may be strained and used as gravy.

4 boneless pork chops
flour for dredging
2 tablespoons canola oil
* 1 cup sweet onion sauce, pg. 20
water

MAKES 4 SERVINGS

use:

• sweet onion sauce, pg. 20

A rushed late-night supper will usually call for minimal preparation. With that said, we bring you...

a pork tenderloin both sweet and sour

In a medium sauté pan, combine all ingredients and simmer until juice has reduced by $1/3$. Serve hot over rice.

* 2 cups cubed pork tenderloin, pg. 39
$1/2$ cup sliced water chestnuts
$1/2$ cup broccoli florets
$1/4$ cup soy sauce
1 tablespoon brown sugar
$1/4$ cup orange juice
dash sherry, optional

MAKES 4 SERVINGS

use:
• pork tenderloin, pg. 39

Scratch-cooking has gone the way of the Ponderosa. Prepare this breakfast on the weekend and heat it on a hurried weekday morning. Saddle up.

cowboy sausage and gravy

In a empty clean jar or plastic food container, shake flour and water to blend. Heat milk in a medium saucepan and add sausage, flour and water mixture. Cook until mixture has thickened. Season with salt and pepper. Remove from heat and spoon gravy over smashed potatoes.

3 tablespoons flour
1/2 cup water
2 cups milk
* 1 lb. cooked sausage, pg. 40
salt and pepper to taste
* 2 cups smashed potatoes,
   warmed, pg. 55

use:

• naked sausage, pg. 40

• smashed potatoes, pg. 55

MAKES 4 SERVINGS

If there happened to be a side dish of warm applesauce dusted with cinnamon sitting on the table, it's safe to assume there would be few objections.

a casserole made with sausage

Heat oven to 350°. Grease a baking dish and set aside. In a large bowl, beat eggs well. Add milk and bread cubes. Set aside to allow bread to soften. Combine $1/2$ cup of the cheese, sausage, mushrooms, red pepper and parsley with bread cube mixture. Pour into baking dish. Top with remaining cheese and a dash of paprika. Bake until cheese has melted, approximately 45 minutes.

6 eggs
2 cups milk
$2^{1}/_{2}$ cups stale bread cubes
* 1 lb. cooked sausage, pg. 40
1 cup grated cheddar cheese
1 cup sliced mushrooms
$1/_{4}$ cup diced red bell pepper
2 tablespoons minced fresh flat-leaf
   parsley
dash paprika

use:

• naked sausage, pg. 40

MAKES 4-6 SERVINGS

A pot of hot tea might go with more than just jam and bread. There is only one way to find out.

ham and bread

In a saucepan, heat cream and ham. Remove from heat and spoon over slices of toast. Place butter in saucepan and add mushrooms. Sauté lightly. In a small bowl, whisk eggs and milk together. Pour into saucepan and stir until scrambled. Spoon over toast and serve immediately. Garnish with parsley.

2 tablespoons heavy cream
* 1 cup minced ham, pg. 44
4 slices bread, toasted
1 tablespoon butter
$1/4$ cup sliced mushrooms
8 eggs
2 tablespoons milk
1 tablespoon chopped fresh flat-leaf
   parsley for garnish

MAKES 4 SERVINGS

use:
• honey-mustard glazed ham, pg. 44

Try grilling or broiling a quesadilla. As long as the cheese melts, the method you choose is not unsound.

brimming with beef quesadillas

Using a sharp knife, carefully cut open one side of each pita. Fill each with $1/2$ cup steak and $1/4$ cup cheese. Place in a nonstick skillet and heat until cheese melts. Press with a spatula to flatten. Garnish with alfalfa sprouts. Serve with black beans and guacamole.

4 pita breads
* 2 cups cooked thinly sliced steak, pg. 42
1 cup shredded Monterey Jack cheese
alfalfa sprouts for garnish
black beans and guacamole as accompaniments

use:
•honey-mustard steaks, pg. 42

MAKES 4 SERVINGS

Corned beef hash is, by turn-of-the-century standards, considered reckless breakfast food. Its heartiness suffices to serve at supper.

a quiche of corned beef

Heat oven to 375°. Process chunks of corned beef in a food processor workbowl until small pieces. Mix onion with corned beef hash. Lightly grease a glass 9-inch pie dish. Press cold mashed potatoes into pie dish to form a crust. Spread corned beef mixture on top. Bake for 25 minutes or until lightly browned. Remove from oven. Crack eggs carefully over top of quiche, taking care not to break yolks. Return to oven until egg whites have cooked completely, about 4 minutes. Season with salt and pepper. Serve immediately.

* 2 cups cooked chunks corned beef, pg. 43
1 small onion, minced
* 2 cups cooked smashed potatoes, pg. 55
4 large eggs
salt and pepper to taste

use:

• corned beef, pg. 43

• smashed potatoes, pg. 55

MAKES 4 SERVINGS

Maybe red flannel hash gets its name because the chopped red, pink, white and grey ingredients resemble a heavy winter pajama set.

red flannel hash

Heat oven to 350°. In a large bowl, combine all ingredients and transfer to a lightly greased baking dish. Bake until golden brown, about 35 minutes.

* 1$^1/_2$ cups chopped cooked corned beef , pg. 43
1 yellow onion, chopped
6 beets, cooked and chopped
* 6 potatoes, cooked and chopped, pg. 27
$^1/_4$ cup canola oil
$^1/_4$ cup water
salt and pepper to taste

use:

• boiled potatoes, pg. 27

• corned beef, pg. 43

MAKES 4-6 SERVINGS

It is fitting, isn't it, that "steak," the most choice of all meats, is put in the same category as that rascal, Caesar.

Caesar steak salad

In a salad bowl, add steak, potatoes, green onions, red pepper, croutons and lettuce. Toss to blend. Pour dressing over salad, using more if desired. Toss to coat well. Garnish with parsley. Serve immediately.

* 2 cups cold, cooked thinly sliced steak, pg. 42
* 2 cold boiled potatoes, peeled and diced, pg. 27
4 green onions, diced
$1/2$ roasted bell red pepper, seeded, peeled and cut in strips
* $1/2$ cup croutons, pg. 26
romaine lettuce, in pieces
* $1/2$-1 cup Caesar salad dressing, pg. 25
fresh flat-leaf parsley for garnish

use:

• hail Caesar dressing, pg. 25

• boiled potatoes, pg. 27

• honey-mustard steaks, pg. 42

• garlic crunch croutons, pg. 26

MAKES 4-6 SERVINGS

The elements of true Sicilian cooking stand tall and proud –
raisins, anchovies, olives and fresh lemon juice.
But of course, one must not forget to include the olive oil.

why is it Sicilian pasta?

Add oil to a sauté pan. Add red pepper and sauté until tender. Add olives, pine nuts and anchovies. Heat thoroughly. Add sliced beef, lemon juice, salt and pepper. Stir well. Remove from heat. In a large pot, bring water to a boil. Add pasta to boiling water and cook for about 3 minutes. The pasta should be firm to the bite, just tender. Drain pasta and spoon onto serving platter. Pour beef over pasta.

3 tablespoons virgin olive oil
1 red bell pepper, seeded and cut
   into strips
12 pitted kalamata olives
$\frac{1}{4}$ cup pine nuts
8 anchovy fillets, cut into pieces
* 2 cups cooked thinly sliced beef,
   pg. 37
1 tablespoon fresh lemon juice
salt and pepper to taste
* 1 lb. fresh pasta, pg. 16

use:
• pasta dough, pg. 16
• roast beef, pg. 37

MAKES 4 SERVINGS

You may want to tie a lobster bib around your neck when you eat this wrap. It is stuffed full of beef and cheese, ingredients designed to make a happy mess.

shredded beef wraps

Heat oven to 350°. Layer beef, rice, beans, cheese, tomato sauce and oregano on flour tortillas. Fold tortillas burrito-style around filling. Wrap in foil and heat until cheese melts.

* 2 cups cooked shredded beef, pg. 37
* 2 cups cooked rice, pg. 32
1 can (15 oz.) kidney beans, rinsed and drained
1 cup shredded mozzarella cheese
1 cup tomato sauce
1 tablespoon minced fresh oregano
4 large flour tortillas

use:
• basic rice, pg. 32
• roast beef, pg. 37

MAKES 4 SERVINGS

The wrap's popularity is outliving the trend it created.
It is here to stay, providing an entire meal in minutes.

chicken wraps with a whole lot of citrus

In a medium saucepan, combine rice and soy sauce over low heat. Add chicken, salsa and pinto beans. Stir to combine. Heat thoroughly. Place tortillas on a flat surface. Cover each tortilla with one layer of lettuce. Spoon chicken mixture onto the center of tortilla. Fold sides in and bottom up to close.

* 2 cups cooked white rice, pg. 32
2 tablespoons soy sauce
* 2 cups cubed roasted chicken pieces, pg. 49
* 1 cup citrus salsa, pg. 23
1 can (15 oz.) pinto beans, rinsed and drained
4 large flour tortillas
lettuce leaves

use:
• basic rice, pg. 32
• roasted chicken, pg. 49
• sunny citrus salsa, pg. 23

MAKES 4 SERVINGS

If you crave the secret spices of the Middle East, this recipe may take your palate and mind to such a place.

chicken stew with garbanzos

In a skillet over medium-high heat, sauté onion and garlic until almost translucent. Add chicken pieces, white wine, mint and chicken stock. Cover and simmer until chicken is heated through. Add garbanzo beans and continue cooking until thoroughly heated. Season with salt and pepper. Garnish with chopped parsley.

1 large yellow onion, chopped
2 cloves garlic, minced
2 teaspoons paprika
$1/2$ teaspoon cayenne pepper
* 2 cups roasted chicken pieces, pg. 49
1 cup white wine
1 teaspoon chopped fresh mint
1 cup chicken stock
1 can (15 oz.) garbanzo beans, rinsed and drained
salt and pepper to taste
2 teaspoons chopped flat-leaf fresh parsley for garnish

use:
• roasted chicken, pg. 49

MAKES 4 SERVINGS

There is always a way to vary chicken salad.
This particular version fuses Middle Eastern flavors with
ingredients common to Asian cuisine.

Far East salad

In a large bowl, whisk tahini, soy sauce, garlic, vinegar or lemon juice, sugar, salt, pepper and cayenne until smooth. Add cubed chicken, cubed cucumber, water chestnuts, green onions and cilantro. Stir to coat well. Transfer to individual plates or a serving platter. Garnish with fried chow mein noodles.

2 tablespoons tahini
1 tablespoon soy sauce
$1/4$ teaspoon minced garlic
1 tablespoon rice wine vinegar
   or lemon juice
$1/4$ teaspoon sugar
salt and pepper to taste
dash cayenne pepper
* 2 cups cubed roasted chicken
   pieces, pg. 49
1 cucumber, peeled and cubed
$1/4$ cup chopped or sliced water
   chestnuts
1 tablespoon chopped green onions
1 tablespoon minced cilantro leaves
$1/2$ cup fried chow mein noodles for
   garnish

use:
• roasted chicken, pg. 49

MAKES 4 SERVINGS

Sometimes it's so difficult to get the smell of mustard off of your hands. But you won't have that problem here, unless you were to make this into a sandwich...

creamy chicken salad

In a large bowl, combine all ingredients and mix well. Cover and refrigerate for 3 hours, or until flavors have had a chance to incorporate. Serve over spinach and garnish with sprouts.

* 2 cups cubed cooked chicken, pg. 48 or pg. 49
1/2 cup petit peas, drained
1/2 cup mayonnaise
1 teaspoon lemon juice
1/4 teaspoon Dijon mustard
1/2 teaspoon minced fresh flat-leaf parsley
1/2 cup diced celery
1/2 cup whole pecans
1/2 roasted red bell pepper, seeds and ribs removed, diced
salt and pepper to taste
dash cayenne pepper
1 pkg. (8 oz.) baby spinach
alfalfa sprouts for garnish

use:
• chicken in a pot, pg. 48 or
• roasted chicken, pg. 49

MAKES 4 SERVINGS

In less than half an hour you could be sitting down to dinner. Tempting? If it is, you know what to make – tomato chicken penne.

tomato chicken penne

Cook pasta according to directions until firm. Lightly sauté onion in a tablespoon of oil until translucent. Add garlic and cook briefly. Add tomatoes, red pepper flakes and oregano and cook until reduced. Add chicken pieces. Simmer until chicken is heated through. Drain pasta and transfer to serving platter or individual plates. Top pasta with sauce. Garnish with parsley and shavings of Parmesan cheese.

8 oz. penne pasta
1 small yellow onion, minced
1 tablespoon olive oil
2 cloves garlic, finely minced
3 cups roughly chopped
    fresh tomatoes
dash red pepper flakes
1 tablespoon chopped fresh oregano
* 2 cups cubed roasted chicken
    pieces, pg. 49
1 tablespoon chopped fresh flat-leaf
    parsley
Parmesan cheese, shaved for
    garnish

MAKES 4 SERVINGS

use:

• roasted chicken, pg. 49

Show off your wedding gift. You remember? That shallow casserole that mother gave you? You'll appreciate it more when you see it filled with steaming chicken.

chicken piccata

Lightly season chicken pieces with salt and pepper. Heat oil in a large sauté pan. Add chicken pieces and sauté until heated through. Add mushroom soup. Simmer for about 10 minutes uncovered, or until sauce has thickened. Stir in parsley and lemon juice. Serve over pasta or rice with a bounteous amount of sauce.

* 2 cups cubed roasted chicken pieces, pg. 49
salt and pepper to taste
3 tablespoons olive oil
* 2 cups mushroom soup, pg. 56
1 tablespoon minced fresh flat-leaf parsley
1-2 tablespoons lemon juice

use:
• roasted chicken, pg. 49
• mushroom and caramelized onion soup, pg. 56

MAKES 4 SERVINGS

Pita sandwiches can always be served cold. Rebel; warm these and they become a different meal entirely.

honey-mustard chicken pitas

Heat oven to 400°. In a large bowl, combine chicken, walnuts, apple, cheese and green onions. Thin honey mustard with apple juice. Carefully cut open one side of each pita bread and spoon $1/4$ of the chicken mixture into each pita. Place on a baking sheet and heat until cheese has melted, about 10 minutes. Remove and transfer to individual plates. Garnish with sprouts and serve immediately.

* 2 cups diced roasted chicken, pg. 49
$1/2$ cup chopped walnuts
$1/2$ cup seeded, chopped apple
$1/2$ cup shredded sharp cheddar cheese
2 tablespoons chopped green onions
* $1/2$ cup honey mustard, pg. 19
1 tablespoon apple juice
4 whole wheat pita breads
1 cup alfalfa sprouts for garnish

use:
• honey mustard, pg. 19
• roasted chicken pg. 49

MAKES 4 SERVINGS

If I'm not mistaken, that was a dash of Creole seasoning, wasn't it? A perennial favorite is given a new twist.

Creole ham casserole

Heat oven to 350°. Bring a large pot of water to a boil. Add macaroni and cook until tender, about 8 minutes; drain. In a large bowl, beat eggs until blended. Whisk to combine milk, parsley, Creole seasoning, salt and pepper. Grease a casserole or baking dish with butter. Add a layer of macaroni to baking dish. Top with a layer of cheese. Add a layer of ham. Repeat layers until all ingredients have been used. Pour milk mixture over top. Bake until top is golden brown and bubbly, about 30 minutes.

8 oz. elbow macaroni
2 large eggs
1½ cups milk
1 tablespoon minced fresh flat-leaf parsley
¼ teaspoon Creole seasoning
salt and pepper to taste
1 tablespoon butter
8 oz. cheddar cheese, shredded
* 2 cups minced ham, pg. 44

use:
• honey-mustard glazed ham, pg. 44

MAKES 4 SERVINGS

Just precisely when did families stop serving meat loaf?
Has "meat" become the villain? Call it "pink" and it is nice again.
Lace slabs of bread with this robust filling.

pink loaf

Heat oven to 350°. Grease a baking dish. Combine all ingredients in a large bowl. Form into a loaf shape and transfer to a baking dish. Press firmly together. Coat with plum sauce. Bake for about 1 1/2 hours, basting with more plum sauce periodically. Remove from oven. Let rest a few minutes before serving.

*2 cups minced ham, pg. 44
1 lb. ground round
1 cup breadcrumbs
2 tablespoons chopped onion
2 tablespoons chopped celery
1 tablespoon chopped fresh parsley
1 egg, beaten
* 1/2 cup plum sauce, pg. 24

use:

• plum sauce, pg. 24

• honey-mustard glazed ham, pg. 44

MAKES 6-8 SERVINGS

"Tradition" often implies "time-consuming." At last, a recipe for a traditional version of stuffed cabbage that minimizes your work.

unstuffed cabbage

In a large bowl, mix turkey with rice. Form into meatballs. In a large pot, layer onion, cabbage, sauerkraut, meatballs and tomatoes. Season with salt, pepper and paprika. Simmer covered for about 2 hours. Remove from heat and serve.

* $\frac{1}{2}$ recipe for turkey patties, pg. 52
1 tablespoon white rice
1 large yellow onion, sliced
1 head cabbage, cut into 1-inch strips
1 pkg. (1 lb.) sauerkraut
1 can (14$\frac{1}{2}$ oz.) peeled tomatoes
salt and pepper to taste
paprika to taste
water

MAKES 6-8 SERVINGS

use:
• turkey burgers, pg. 52

This soup is both healthy and filling –
just add crusty bread for a complete meal.

meatball soup

In a stockpot, heat oil and add onion. Sauté over low heat until translucent. Add garlic and sauté briefly. Add broth, vegetables and meatballs. Simmer for about 15 minutes. Season with salt and pepper and serve immediately.

2 tablespoons vegetable oil
1 onion, thinly sliced
1 clove garlic, minced
4 cups chicken broth
2 cups assorted cooked vegetables
* 1 recipe cooked turkey meatballs,
   pg. 102
salt and pepper to taste

MAKES 4 SERVINGS

use:
• turkey meatballs, pg. 102

Turkey is the new "old reliable." And if you keep a stash of these in your freezer, you will never be at a loss for what to serve for dinner.

turkey meatballs

Form turkey mixture into balls the size of apricots. Heat oil in a skillet. Sauté meatballs over medium heat until golden brown. Makes about 20 meatballs. Cool and store in an airtight container or use immediately.

* $\frac{1}{2}$ recipe for turkey patties, pg. 52
olive oil for sautéing

see:

• turkey burgers, pg. 52

• meatball soup, pg. 101

• sweet and sour meatballs, pg. 103

• the Russians are coming meatballs,

   pg. 104

MAKES 4-6 SERVINGS

The sauce tastes so familiar. Chinese take-out from last week?
Plum sauce turns Italy into Asia.
Wouldn't fried rice be great with this?

sweet and sour meatballs

Heat meatballs if necessary. Heat plum sauce in a small saucepan. Transfer meatballs to a serving platter and pour plum sauce over meatballs. Serve immediately.

* 1 recipe cooked turkey meatballs, pg. 102
* 1 cup plum sauce, pg. 24

use:

• plum sauce, pg. 24

• turkey meatballs, pg. 102

MAKES 4-6 SERVINGS

Slurp a warm bowl of this and you'll have the sustenance you'll need to make it through the harsh Siberian winter or the one where you live.

the Russians are coming meatballs

Heat meatballs, if necessary. In a saucepan, heat sour cream and chicken broth. Stir to combine completely. Transfer meatballs to a serving platter. Spoon sour cream sauce over meatballs, season generously with salt and pepper and serve immediately.

* 1 recipe cooked turkey meatballs, pg. 102
2 cups sour cream
1/4 cup chicken broth
salt and pepper to taste

use:

• turkey meatballs, pg. 102

MAKES 4-6 SERVINGS

The chicken sandwich was so wonderful.
But it wasn't served on the normal white bread.
Instead, it came wedged in a handy Middle Eastern bread.

pockets of chicken

Heat broiler. Cut pita bread on the side to separate layers. In a bowl, combine chicken, avocado, green onions, cheese and olives. Stir to combine. Stuff equal portions of chicken mixture into each pita. Place pitas on a baking sheet and place under broiler. Heat until cheese has melted. Remove from oven and garnish with sprouts. Serve immediately.

4 pita breads
* 1/2 remaining meat from café chicken, diced, pg. 46
1 ripe avocado, peeled and diced
2 green onions, chopped
1 cup shredded sharp cheddar cheese
1/4 cup chopped black olives
1/2 cup alfalfa sprouts for garnish

MAKES 4 SERVINGS

use:
• café chicken, pg. 46

The small gourmet olives stuffed with marinated garlic or pimien-tos do exist outside the cocktail circuit. They have the strange power of changing any food to a new ethnicity. The Southwest?

down at the café ranchero salad

Cut garlic in half. In a salad bowl, rub garlic in bottom of bowl and discard used clove. In a small bowl, whisk oil, vinegar, lime juice, cayenne, salt and pepper. Add remaining ingredients to salad bowl and pour dressing on top. Toss to coat. Cover and refrigerate until ready to use.

1 clove garlic
1/2 cup olive oil
1/4 cup apple cider vinegar
2 tablespoons lime juice
dash cayenne pepper
salt and pepper to taste
* 1 cup diced meat from café chicken, pg. 47
1/2 cup green pimiento olives
1/2 cup grated Monterey Jack cheese
1/4 cup diced, roasted red bell peppers
1 pkg. (12 oz.) baby greens
4 thick slices sourdough bread, toasted, in large cubes
1 tablespoon minced fresh cilantro
1 cup halved cherry tomatoes
1/4 cup canned pinto beans, rinsed and drained

use:
• café chicken, pg. 47

MAKES 4-6 SERVINGS

Sitting outside on the patio in the late afternoon. Summer takes away the appetite. The sun is going down. A light supper, maybe a frittata tonight... That would be just splendid.

an asparagus frittata tonight

Heat broiler. Cut asparagus into bite-sized pieces. Heat butter in a 10- or 12-inch heavy ovenproof skillet. Add minced onion and sauté until translucent. Reduce heat to low. Beat eggs just until blended. Add minced basil to eggs. Pour eggs over onions. Add asparagus. Cook until eggs are just set, but still custard-like. Sprinkle with Parmesan cheese. Remove skillet from stove and place under broiler until cheese has melted and eggs are set. Loosen frittata and carefully slide onto a serving platter. Season with salt and pepper.

* 8 spears cold asparagus, pg. 33
3 tablespoons butter
1 small onion, minced
7 extra-large eggs
1 tablespoon minced fresh basil
$1/4$ cup grated Parmesan cheese
salt and pepper to taste

MAKES 4-6 SERVINGS

use:

• asparagus, pg. 33

Whose idea was it to serve the salad in a glass bowl?
Clever. All of the colorful layers are visible.

look at the colorful salad

Mix oil, lemon juice, sugar and garlic. Season with salt and pepper. In a large glass bowl, layer bottom of bowl with greens. Layer with chicken, tomatoes, garbanzo beans, cucumber, onion and red pepper. Layer until ingredients are used. Sprinkle Gorgonzola on top and decorate with olives and croutons. Garnish with fresh mint or parsley.

2 tablespoons olive oil
2 tablespoons lemon juice
1 teaspoon sugar
1 clove garlic, minced
salt and pepper to taste
1 pkg. (12 oz.) mixed baby greens
   (spinach, radicchio), torn
* 1 cup chopped cold roasted chicken,
   pg. 49
2 tomatoes, cubed
$1/2$ cup garbanzo beans
$1/2$ cucumber, peeled, seeded and diced
1 small sweet onion, chopped
1 large red bell pepper, seeded and chopped
$1/2$ cup crumbled Gorgonzola cheese
12 nicoise olives
* croutons, pg. 26
$1/4$ cup chopped fresh mint or parsley
   for garnish

use:

• garlic crunch croutons, pg. 26

• roasted chicken, pg. 49

MAKES 4 SERVINGS

Why just limit French toast to Sunday mornings?
Keep that untouched Sunday paper for a weeknight.

baked French toast

In a large bowl, whisk to combine eggs, milk and spices. Place slices of bread in a greased casserole. Pour milk mixture over bread. Cover and refrigerate overnight. The following morning, heat oven to 450°. Spoon strawberries over bread. Top with almonds and sprinkle with sugar. Bake for about 20 minutes or until milk mixture is firm. Remove from oven and allow to rest for several minutes. Serve while still warm.

6 eggs
$^3/_4$ cup milk
dash cinnamon
dash ground nutmeg
dash ground ginger
* 8 slices bread, cut into 1-inch
  slices, pg. 31
2 cups fresh strawberries, hulled and
  cut in half
$^1/_4$ cup slivered almonds
dash sugar

MAKES 4 SERVINGS

use:
• peasant bread, pg. 31

The soup sops up the bread rather than the reverse.
You may need to run and grab a baguette.
The lure to soak up leftover juices is daunting.

bread soup

Heat oil in a large stockpot. Add onion and sauté until almost translucent. Add garlic and sauté briefly. Add tomatoes and cook just until tender. Remove pot from heat and allow to stand for 1 hour. After waiting period, add chicken stock to pot and simmer. Add basil and bread chunks and serve immediately in large bowls with fresh Parmesan.

3 tablespoons olive oil
1 large onion, minced
4 cloves garlic, minced
2 lb. ripe tomatoes, peeled, seeded and chopped
6 cups chicken broth
$1/4$ cup fresh basil, cut into thin strips
* 1 lb. crusty bread, cut into chunks, pg. 31
freshly grated Parmesan cheese

use:
• peasant bread, pg. 31

MAKES 6-8 SERVINGS

They say it was an accident that the peel was left on the apples. But what a splash of extra color the salad has!

composed shrimp and apple salad

In a large bowl, whisk mayonnaise, lemon juice, tarragon, salt, pepper and cayenne. Add remaining ingredients except tomatoes and lettuce and stir well to coat. Cover and refrigerate for several hours. Place lettuce leaves on individual plates or a serving platter. Spoon shrimp salad onto lettuce leaves. Garnish with cherry tomatoes.

$1/2$ cup mayonnaise
1 tablespoon lemon juice
1 teaspoon chopped fresh tarragon
salt and pepper to taste
dash cayenne pepper
* 3 cups leftover shrimp, cooked and cut into bite-size pieces, pg. 57
1 tablespoon capers
1 cup diced celery
$1/2$ cup kalamata olives
1 cup chopped red apple
4 green onions, sliced
several large lettuce leaves
16 cherry tomatoes

use:
• wine and rosemary shrimp, pg. 57

MAKES 6-8 SERVINGS

Honey, the guests always love those shrimp appetizers.
Why don't you make a platter of those to start?

# of course, the baked shrimp

Heat oven to 350°. Grease a baking dish or casserole. Heat olive oil in a sauté pan. Add shallots and red pepper. Sauté until tender. Stir in flour and gradually add milk. Stir in dry mustard. Add shrimp to baking dish. Pour onion mixture in casserole. Mix tarragon with breadcrumbs and sprinkle over top of shrimp. Bake for about 30 minutes or until sauce has reduced. Season with salt and pepper and serve immediately.

$1/4$ cup olive oil
2 shallots, minced
1 red bell pepper, seeded and diced
2 tablespoons flour
2 cups milk
$1/4$ teaspoon dry mustard
* 2 cups cooked shrimp, pg. 57
1 teaspoon dried tarragon
1 cup dried breadcrumbs
salt and pepper to taste

MAKES 4 SERVINGS

use:
• wine and rosemary shrimp, pg. 57

It is so confusing – the difference between a crostini, panini and bruschetta. What are they, again?

fresh mozzarella crostini

Heat oven to 400°. In a small bowl, mix garlic with 1 tablespoon oil, tomato paste and basil. Place bread slices on a baking sheet. Using a pastry brush, coat the top side of each piece of bread with olive oil. Spread tomato mixture on each piece of bread. Top each with a slice of mozzarella. Bake for about 8 to10 minutes or until cheese has melted. Serve immediately.

2 cloves garlic, minced
1/4 cup chopped fresh basil
3 tablespoons olive oil
1 tablespoon sun-dried tomato paste
* 8 slices peasant bread, pg. 31
1 lb. fresh mozzarella cheese, sliced
salt and pepper to taste

use:
• peasant bread, pg. 31

MAKES 4 SERVINGS

One tends to forget that sesame seeds are sold in boxes at the grocery store. You must not forget to use them, though. Maybe this recipe will serve as a reminder.

sesame asparagus salad

In a small bowl, whisk tamari sauce, sesame oil or tahini, lemon juice and sugar to combine. Add asparagus and stir to coat well. Cover and refrigerate until ready to serve. Place greens on individual plates or a serving platter. Spoon asparagus mixture on top of greens and decorate with orange sections. Garnish with sesame seeds.

2 tablespoons tamari sauce
1 teaspoon sesame oil or tahini
1 teaspoon lemon juice
1 teaspoon sugar
* 2 cups cooked asparagus, in
   bite-size pieces, pg. 33
1 pkg. (12 oz.) baby greens
1 can (6.5 oz.) mandarin oranges,
   drained
sesame seeds for garnish

MAKES 4 SERVINGS

use:
• asparagus, pg. 33

Why is an open-faced sandwich much more
visually elegant than a normal sandwich?

yellow pepper bruschetta

Toast bread. Lightly rub garlic clove over bread for flavor. Brush lightly with olive oil. Place on individual plates. Spoon sauce on toast and serve immediately.

* 8 slices crusty bread, pg. 31
1-2 cloves garlic
olive oil for brushing
* 1 cup mellow yellow sauce, pg.34

MAKES 4 SERVINGS

use:

• peasant bread, pg. 31

• mellow yellow sauce, pg. 34

Keep the oil hot and try not to turn the polenta
more than once. This will prevent the slices from absorbing
excess oil. The less oil, the more polenta you can justify to eat.

a slice or two of fried polenta

Pour oil about 1 inch deep in skillet and heat until hot, but not smoking. Carefully transfer polenta slices to hot oil. Fry until golden brown on both sides. Remove immediately and drain on several layers of paper towels. Serve immediately. Drizzle with tomato salsa.

canola oil for frying
* 1 recipe polenta, pg. 28
* tomato salsa, pg. 22

use:

• polenta, pg. 28

• tomato salsa, pg. 22

MAKES 6 SERVINGS

Fried rice isn't a treat restricted to the take-out menu.
Don't say you can't make it "as good" without trying first.
You may surprise yourself.

pork fried rice

In a large sauté pan over high heat, heat oil.
Add rice and onion. Stir-fry for a few minutes.
Add pork and vegetables. Make a well in the center of the pan. Pour eggs into the center and stir-fry until scrambled. Combine gently with rice mixture. Add broth and soy sauce and stir. Season with salt and pepper.

2 tablespoons canola oil
* 4 cups cold, cooked rice, pg. 32
1 small onion, minced
* 1/2 cup diced cooked pork, pg. 38
* 1/4 cup cooked carrots
   Marrakesh, pg. 133
1/2 cup bean sprouts
2 eggs, beaten
1/4 cup chicken broth
1 tablespoon soy sauce
salt and pepper to taste

use:
• basic rice, pg. 32
• Montreal pork roast, pg. 38
• cooked carrots Marrakesh, pg. 133

MAKES 4 SERVINGS

It's a comfort food you probably heard mentioned in a story somehow tied together with the old "walking to school 10 miles in the snow" or "my grandmother used to make the best..."

rice pudding

Heat oven to 325° and grease a baking dish. In a medium bowl, mix all ingredients and pour into baking dish. Bake for 1 hour, or until pudding has thickened. Chill until ready to serve.

butter, for greasing
* 2 cups cooked rice, pg. 32
1$\frac{1}{3}$ cups milk
$\frac{1}{4}$ cup sugar
3 eggs, beaten
$\frac{1}{4}$ cup chopped dried blueberries, dried cherries or dried apricots
$\frac{1}{2}$ teaspoon vanilla extract

use:
• basic rice, pg. 32

MAKES 8 SERVINGS

Using canned beans instead of dried allows this recipe to be a much quicker version than the traditional.

white bean soup

In a medium stockpot, add navy beans, chicken broth and ham. Simmer for 30 minutes to allow flavors to blend. Add celery, potato, green beans, garlic and onion. Simmer for 1 hour. Season with salt and pepper. Garnish with parsley and croutons.

1 cup canned navy beans, rinsed and drained
4 cups chicken broth
* $^1/_2$ cup cubed ham, pg. 44
$^1/_4$ cup diced celery
1 potato, peeled and cubed
1 cup chopped fresh green beans
1 clove garlic, minced
1 cup minced onion
salt and pepper to taste
chopped fresh flat-leaf parsley for garnish
* croutons for garnish, pg. 26

use:
• garlic crunch croutons, pg. 26
• honey-mustard glazed ham, pg. 44

MAKES 8 SERVINGS

Have you ever wanted a bowl of chowder and a hunk of good sourdough bread on a foggy evening? Try this.

a little hot corn chowder

In a stockpot, sauté bacon until it softens. Add onion and continue cooking until lightly browned. You may pour off most of the fat, if you desire, but retain some. Add celery and potatoes. Cook until celery is tender. Add corn, milk, salt, pepper and cayenne. Simmer until corn is thoroughly heated. Serve with a garnish of fresh parsley.

4 slices bacon
1 onion, diced
1/4 cup diced celery
*1 cup diced cooked potatoes, pg. 27
* 2 cups cooked corn kernels, pg. 33
2 cups milk
salt and pepper to taste
dash cayenne pepper
water
1 tablespoon chopped fresh flat-leaf parsley

use:
• boiled potatoes, pg. 27
• corn, pg. 33

MAKES 4 SERVINGS

Shuck your corn well; no stray threads allowed in this beautiful salad. Subtle colors – buttery yellow and pearl white from both corn varieties and soft green sugar peas are reminders of the plains states and their subdued landscape.

sweet corn and sugar pea salad

Cut corn off cob using a sharp knife. In a large bowl, whisk oil, shallots, lemon juice, mint, sugar, salt, pepper and cayenne to combine. Add corn, sugar peas and peppers and stir to combine. Cover and refrigerate for several hours for flavors to meld. Serve on large lettuce leaves.

* 4 ears cooked corn, pg. 33
2 tablespoons canola oil
2 shallots, diced
2 tablespoons lemon juice
1 tablespoon minced fresh mint
1 teaspoon sugar
salt and pepper to taste
dash cayenne pepper
1 cup sugar peas, blanched
1 roasted red bell pepper, seeded, peeled and diced
6 large lettuce leaves

use:

• corn, pg. 33

MAKES 4-6 SERVINGS

This is food for the party or after the party –
serve with pita bread and a glass of wine or two.

baba ghanoush

Spoon eggplant into a food processor workbowl. Add remaining ingredients. Process until smooth, adding a bit more oil if necessary. Correct seasonings. Transfer to a bowl. Cover and refrigerate overnight if possible.

* 1 eggplant, roasted, pg. 27
1-2 cloves garlic
$\frac{1}{4}$ cup minced onion
3 tablespoons tahini
$\frac{1}{4}$ cup lemon juice
$\frac{1}{4}$ cup minced fresh flat-leaf parsley
2 tablespoons olive oil
salt to taste
cayenne pepper to taste

use:
• roasted eggplant, pg. 27

MAKES 3 CUPS

They offered me a bowl of this wonderful soup before
I wandered out into the cold night. It saw me through the storm.

one potato, two potato soup

In a stockpot over medium heat, add potato water. In a sauté pan, heat oil and add onion. Sauté until translucent. Add garlic and sauté briefly. Place potatoes, onions and garlic in a food processor workbowl; process until smooth. Transfer potato mixture to stockpot and stir well to blend. Add Creole seasoning and milk. Add more water if soup is too thick. Simmer for about 10 minutes or until desired thickness. Season with salt and pepper. Add parsley. Remove from heat and serve immediately.

* cooking water from boiled
  potatoes, pg. 27
1 tablespoon vegetable oil
1 large yellow onion, diced
2 cloves garlic, minced
* 2 lb. cooked potatoes, pg. 27
1/4 teaspoon Creole seasoning
1 cup milk
salt and pepper to taste
1 tablespoon minced fresh flat-leaf
  parsley

use:
• boiled potatoes, pg. 27

MAKES 4-6 SERVINGS

There are still people who wake up to the sound of a rooster, who put in a full day of labor, who cook in an iron skillet and who draw water from the well. All of that work is going to make someone very hungry.

farmhouse potato cakes

In a large bowl, mix potatoes, vegetables, breadcrumbs or matzo meal, egg white, salt, pepper and green onions together to form a firm mixture. Make patties. Heat oil in a skillet. Sauté patties until golden brown. Drain on paper towels. Serve immediately.

* 1 cup smashed potatoes, pg. 55
1 cup cooked vegetables
  (carrots, peas, broccoli, squash)
1 cup dried breadcrumbs or matzo
  meal
1 egg white
salt and pepper to taste
2 green onions, chopped, optional
2 tablespoons canola oil

use:
• smashed potatoes, pg. 55

MAKES 4 SERVINGS

Let's face it, it's hard to come close to cooking those incredible fries at the fast food joints. So, why even try? There's a reason these are called "home fries." They are simple, taste homemade and are awash with flavor. They can be eaten at breakfast, lunch or dinner. Pass the ketchup, please.

home fries

In a large frying pan with a nonstick surface, heat oil to cover bottom of pan to about $1/8$-inch. Add potatoes and onion. Sauté until potatoes are nicely browned and crisp. Add paprika, salt and pepper to taste.

canola or peanut oil for frying
* 3 cups cold boiled potatoes, sliced, pg. 27
1 onion, sliced
dash paprika
salt and pepper to taste

MAKES 4 SERVINGS

use:
• boiled potatoes, pg. 27

We all have those days where all we want for dinner is a bowl of cereal or something maybe a little sweet. A piping hot bowl of these will take care of that odd craving. Serve with ham, bacon or a hearty bowl of oatmeal.

apple mash

n a mixing bowl, beat ingredients together. Serve immediately.

* 2 cups smashed potatoes, warmed, pg. 55
1 cup chunky applesauce, warmed
1 tablespoon butter, melted

MAKES 4 SERVINGS

use:
• smashed potatoes, pg. 55

This traditional favorite has a new look and taste.
Make mother-in-law's potato salad when she visits, and sneak
this one in when she has her back turned.

bacon potato salad

In a large skillet over medium-high heat, fry bacon until crisp. Remove and drain on paper towels. In a bowl, whisk vinegar, oil, garlic, sugar, salt and pepper. Arrange potato slices in center of individual plates. Top each serving with 2 strips of bacon broken into several pieces. Cut green section of each green onion into lengthwise strips, taking care not to cut green onion apart. Lay one green onion on top of each serving of potatoes. Sprinkle with parsley. Spoon dressing on top of each serving.

8 slices bacon
1 tablespoon raspberry vinegar
$1/4$ cup canola oil
1 clove garlic, minced
1 tablespoon sugar
salt and pepper to taste
*2 cups sliced cooked boiled
   potatoes, pg. 27
4 green onions
1 tablespoon chopped fresh flat-leaf
   parsley

use:
• boiled potatoes, pg. 27

MAKES 4 SERVINGS

Since gnocchi is a traditional recipe in Italian homes, there are almost as many recipes as there are families. This version is slightly eccentric. There is no psychological correlation between the family it came from and its uniqueness.

tomato-pesto gnocchi

In a large bowl, mix potatoes, egg, melted butter, flour, salt and pepper. Stir until all ingredients are just incorporated. Do not overbeat. The mixture should be quite stiff. Turn potato mixture out onto a lightly floured piece of plastic wrap and form into a roll. Chill thoroughly until roll is not sticky. Heat oil in a large skillet or saucepan. The oil should be about 3-inches deep. Cut potato roll into 1-inch rounds. Dip rounds into extra flour and carefully place in hot oil. Fry until golden brown. Drain on paper towels and keep warm until ready to serve. Arrange gnocchi on individual plates or a serving platter. Spoon tomato pesto over gnocchi and sprinkle with Parmesan cheese.

* 2 cups smashed potatoes, room temperature, pg. 55
1 egg, beaten
2 tablespoons butter, melted
$1/2$ cup flour
salt and pepper to taste
canola oil for sautéing
extra flour
* $1/2$ cup tomato pesto, pg. 21
1 cup grated Parmesan cheese

use:

• tomato pesto, pg. 21

• smashed potatoes, pg. 55

MAKES 4 SERVINGS

You love anchovies, but nobody else does, right?
Well, if that is the case, all the more for you.
This keeps well refrigerated, so eat up.

anchovy potato salad

In a large bowl, whisk to combine anchovy paste, parsley, lemon juice, zest, garlic and olive oil. Add potatoes and stir to coat well. Season well with salt and pepper and garnish with chopped green onions. Cover with plastic wrap and refrigerate for several hours to let flavors blend.

1 teaspoon anchovy paste
1 tablespoon chopped fresh flat-leaf parsley
1 tablespoon lemon juice
zest of 1 lemon, minced
1 clove garlic, minced
3 tablespoons virgin olive oil
* 2 cups cubed boiled potatoes, pg. 27
salt and pepper to taste
2 green onions, chopped

MAKES 4 SERVINGS

use:

• boiled potatoes, pg. 27

This is so French country that it would be a crime not to serve it out of a ceramic, hand-painted casserole dish. You DO have one with cows painted on the side or with a landscape of the French Provence, right?

spring asparagus gratin

Heat broiler. In a small bowl, combine breadcrumbs and Parmesan cheese. Arrange asparagus spears in a shallow baking dish or casserole. Drizzle with olive oil. Sprinkle with cheese mixture and add salt and pepper. Slide baking dish under broiler and broil until cheese has melted, about 3 minutes.

1 tablespoon dried breadcrumbs
2 tablespoons grated Parmesan cheese
* 1 lb. cooked asparagus, pg. 33
1 tablespoon olive oil
salt and pepper to taste

MAKES 4 SERVINGS

use:
• asparagus, pg. 33

Luckily these boats aren't real; they are so jam-packed with rice and beans that they would likely sink.

zucchini Cajun boats

Heat oven to 350°. Lightly oil a baking dish. Cut zucchini in half and scoop out seeded portion of flesh. Chop and add to rice mixture. Fill zucchini with rice and place in baking dish. Cover with foil and bake until zucchini is tender, about 20 minutes. Remove from oven and let cool slightly. Top with a dollop of yogurt and garnish with fresh mint. Serve immediately.

4 medium zucchini
* $1/2$ recipe red beans and rice, pg. 60
1 cup plain yogurt
chopped fresh mint for garnish

use:
• red beans and rice, pg. 60

MAKES 4 SERVINGS

A sensible side dish. Yes. A classic holiday accompaniment
served in your favorite crystal bowl. Of course.
A plastic container toted to the tailgate party?
I don't see why not. Are these beans suitable for all
of these occasions and more? Yes.

honey-mustard green beans

Heat water to a boil in a medium saucepan. Trim green beans and add to water. Cook for about 6 minutes or until beans are bright green and tender but not limp. Drain and transfer to a bowl. In a small bowl, add honey mustard, a tablespoon of water and oil; whisk to blend. Add more water, if necessary, to reach the consistency of a salad dressing. Pour dressing over beans and ham. Toss to coat. Cover and refrigerate for at least 30 minutes.

1 lb. green beans
* $^1/_4$ cup honey mustard, pg. 20
water for thinning mustard
1 tablespoon canola oil
* 1 cup diced cooked ham, pg. 44

use:

• honey mustard, pg. 20

• honey-mustard glazed ham, pg. 44

MAKES 4 SERVINGS

The road to Marrakesh, starring Hope and Crosby, may never have come to fruition, but these carrots Marrakesh promise to be a blockbuster hit.

carrots Marrakesh

In a small bowl, whisk to combine garlic, lemon juice, oil, herbs and spices. Add carrots and stir to coat well. Add diced ham and raisins and toss to combine.

1 small clove garlic, minced
1 tablespoon lemon juice
2 tablespoons canola oil
1 tablespoon minced fresh mint
1 tablespoon minced fresh flat-leaf parsley
$1/4$ teaspoon ground cumin
$1/4$ teaspoon cinnamon
$1/2$ teaspoon paprika
dash cayenne pepper
salt and pepper to taste
2 cups sliced cooked carrots
* 1 cup diced cooked ham, pg. 35
1 cup raisins

use:
• honey-mustard glazed ham, pg. 35

MAKES 4 SERVINGS

for whenever

Guaranteed, you'll be hard-pressed to find this dynamic duo topping at any pizza place. Do a little searching at the cheese shop for an agreeable cheese.

Gorgonzola and walnut pizza

Heat oven to 450°. Roll dough into desired size and shape on a baking sheet. Arrange walnut pieces on dough. Drizzle with oil. Crumble cheese on top. Sprinkle parsley over cheese. Bake until crust is golden and cheese is melted, about 20 minutes. Serve immediately.

* 1 recipe pizza dough, pg. 13
1/2 cup chopped walnuts
3 tablespoons olive oil
8 oz. Gorgonzola cheese, crumbled
1 teaspoon minced fresh flat-leaf
   parsley
salt and pepper to taste

MAKES ONE 14-INCH PIZZA
OR
4 INDIVIDUAL PIZZETTES

use:
• pizza dough, pg. 13

You will never miss the tomato sauce. Plum, fresh tomatoes give this classic Northern Italian pizza its signature look and taste.

pizza Margherita

Heat oven to 450°. Roll dough into desired size and shape on a baking sheet. Layer with tomato slices and cover tomato slices with whole fresh basil leaves. Sprinkle generously with mozzarella and drizzle with olive oil. Bake until crust is golden and cheese is melted, about 20 minutes. Serve immediately.

*1 recipe pizza dough, pg. 13
2 tomatoes, thinly sliced
12 whole fresh basil leaves
1 cup shredded mozzarella cheese
1-2 tablespoons olive oil

MAKES ONE 14-INCH PIZZA
OR
4 INDIVIDUAL PIZZETTES

use:
• pizza dough, pg. 13

Peppers are deceiving. Normally, red is associated with heat.
Bell peppers, however, break all of the rules.
The brighter the color, the sweeter.

four pepper pizza

Heat oven to 450°. Roll dough into desired size and shape on a baking sheet. Arrange pepper slices on dough. Sprinkle with fresh basil and drizzle with olive oil. Top with sliced fontina and sprinkle with grated Parmesan. Bake until crust is golden and cheese has melted. Serve immediately.

* 1 recipe pizza dough, pg. 13
1 red bell pepper, seeded and sliced
1 orange bell pepper, seeded and sliced
1 yellow bell pepper, seeded and sliced
1 green bell pepper, seeded and sliced
1 tablespoon chopped fresh basil
1-2 tablespoons olive oil
8 oz. Italian fontina cheese, sliced
1/2 cup grated Parmesan cheese

MAKES ONE 14-INCH PIZZA
OR
4 INDIVIDUAL PIZZETTES

use:
• pizza dough, pg. 13

Parma ham is a luxury.
It comes in paper-thin slices and tastes heavenly.

pizza di Parma

Heat oven to 450°. Roll dough into desired size and shape. Heat olive oil in a sauté pan. Add onions and slowly cook over low heat until brown and caramelized. Layer ham on dough. Spoon caramelized onions over ham. Sprinkle with fresh rosemary and mozzarella. Drizzle with a little olive oil. Bake until crust is golden and cheese has melted, about 20 minutes. Serve immediately.

* 1 recipe pizza dough, pg. 13
1 tablespoon olive oil, plus additional for drizzling
1 yellow onion, thinly sliced
8 oz. Parma ham
1/4 cup chopped fresh rosemary
1 cup shredded mozzarella cheese

MAKES ONE 14-INCH PIZZA
OR
4 INDIVIDUAL PIZZETTES

use:

• pizza dough, pg. 13

At the height of summer's bounty, it's possible
to find yellow tomatoes at the market.
Use these for an interesting change.

tricoloré pizza

Heat oven to 450°. Roll dough into desired shape. Brush dough with olive oil. Layer pepper slices on dough followed by tomato slices. Add basil and top with cheese. Bake until crust is golden brown and cheese has melted, about 20 minutes. Serve immediately.

* 1 recipe pizza dough, pg. 13
2 tablespoons olive oil
1 cup roasted red bell pepper slices
2 yellow tomatoes, thinly sliced
fresh basil leaves for garnish
1 cup shredded mozzarella cheese

MAKES ONE 14-INCH PIZZA
OR
4 INDIVIDUAL PIZZETTES

use:
• pizza dough, pg. 13

There is no steadfast rule that says pizza must be made with tomato sauce or even tomatoes. This is a variation on the popular pizza biancas found in gourmet restaurants.

white pizza

Heat oven to 450°. Roll dough into desired shape and size on a baking sheet. Heat I tablespoon of the oil in a sauté pan. Add onion and sauté over low heat until caramelized. Add garlic and sauté briefly. Brush dough with I tablespoon of the oil. Spoon onion mixture over dough. Top with cheese. Sprinkle with parsley and Creole seasoning. Bake until crust is golden brown and cheese has melted, about 20 minutes. Serve immediately.

* 1 recipe pizza dough, pg. 13
2 tablespoons olive oil
1 medium onion, thinly sliced
4 cloves garlic, sliced
1 cup grated Gruyère cheese
1 tablespoon chopped fresh flat-leaf parsley
1/4 teaspoon Creole seasoning, or to taste

MAKES ONE 14-INCH PIZZA
OR
4 INDIVIDUAL PIZZETTES

use:

• pizza dough, pg. 13

New Orleans is both the "Crescent City" as well as the center for creative recipes.

Crescent City pizza

Heat the oven to 450°. Roll dough into desired size and shape on a baking sheet. Layer sausage on dough. Add peppers and cilantro. Top with cheese. Bake until crust is golden brown and cheese has melted, about 20 minutes. Serve immediately.

* 1 recipe pizza dough, pg. 13
1 cup sliced cooked andouille
    sausage
$1/4$ cup diced green bell pepper
$1/4$ cup diced red bell pepper
1 tablespoon minced fresh cilantro
1 cup shredded Monterey Jack
    cheese

MAKES ONE 14-INCH PIZZA
OR
4 INDIVIDUAL PIZZETTES

use:
• pizza dough, pg. 13

The light earth-colored yellow pasta is reminiscent of straw; the green pasta reminds one of new bales of hay.

hay and straw pasta

Add pasta to a large pot of boiling water and cook for about 3 to 4 minutes or until firm to the bite. Remove from heat and drain. Transfer to a serving platter or individual plates. Spoon Gorgonzola cream sauce over pasta. Garnish with freshly ground black pepper and chopped parsley. Serve immediately.

* $^1/_4$ recipe egg pasta, pg. 16
* $^1/_4$ recipe spinach pasta, pg. 17
* 2 cups Gorgonzola cream sauce, warmed, pg. 29
black pepper to taste
chopped fresh flat-leaf parsley for garnish

use:

• egg pasta dough, pg. 16

• spinach pasta dough, pg. 17

• Gorgonzola cream sauce, pg. 29

MAKES 4 SERVINGS

This is excellent on plain egg pasta, but experiment with different colors and tastes. It's lovely on a spinach pasta.

three pepper pasta

Heat olive oil in a sauté pan. Add onion and cook until almost translucent. Reduce heat, add garlic and sauté for about 1 minute. Add peppers. Stir and cover. Simmer for about 5 minutes or until peppers are tender. Add parsley and season with salt and pepper. Boil water in a large pot, add pasta and cook until tender, about 3 minutes. Spoon over pasta.

3 tablespoons olive oil
1 small yellow onion, minced
2 cloves garlic, minced
1 yellow bell pepper, seeded and cut into thin strips
1 orange bell pepper, seeded and cut into thin strips
1 red bell pepper, seeded and cut into thin strips
1 tablespoon chopped fresh parsley
salt and pepper to taste
* 1 lb. fresh pasta, pg. 16

use:
• pasta dough, pg. 16

MAKES 4 SERVINGS

On a summer day when it is too hot to cook,
consider whipping up this easy dish.

summer day pasta

Heat oil in a sauté pan. Add garlic and sauté over medium heat until translucent. Boil water in a large pot, add pasta and cook until tender, about 3 minutes; drain. Add pasta to oil and garlic. Drizzle with lemon juice and toss with parsley and mint. Season with salt and pepper and a dash of red pepper flakes. Serve immediately.

$\frac{1}{2}$ cup olive oil
1 tablespoon minced garlic*
* 1 lb. fresh pasta, pg. 16
$\frac{1}{4}$ cup lemon juice
1 tablespoon minced fresh flat-leaf
  parsley
1 tablespoon minced fresh mint
salt and pepper to taste
red pepper flakes

use:
• pasta dough, pg. 16

MAKES 4 SERVINGS

If you have another pasta shape hiding in the cupboard besides spaghetti, don't let that stop you from making this incredible dish.

spaghetti, eggs and cheese

In a large pot, heat water to a boil. Add pasta and cook until tender. Remove from heat and drain. Transfer pasta to a bowl. To pot, add butter, eggs and cheese. Stir over heat until eggs are scrambled. Transfer cooked pasta to pot and toss to combine. Transfer to individual plates. Season with salt and pepper and garnish with parsley. Serve immediately.

* 1 lb. fresh pasta, pg. 16
2 tablespoons butter
4 eggs, beaten
1 cup grated Parmesan cheese
salt and pepper to taste
fresh flat-leaf parsley for garnish

use:
• pasta dough, pg. 16

MAKES 4 SERVINGS

A large baking dish of lasagne easily serves a room of guests, but it can also be frozen for later use — and reheated in the microwave or oven.

eggplant lasagne

Heat oven to 350°. Boil water in a large pot, add pasta and cook until just tender. Drain and toss with oil to prevent sticking. In a skillet, sauté onion until almost translucent. Add garlic and sauté briefly. Transfer to a bowl. Add roasted eggplant and parsley. Stir to combine. In another bowl, combine ricotta cheese and tofu. Stir to blend. Ladle some spaghetti sauce onto the bottom of a 9-x-13-inch baking dish to prevent lasagne from sticking. Position 1 layer of lasagne on top of sauce. Layer enough eggplant mixture and ricotta mixture on pasta sheet to coat. Coat with a layer of spaghetti sauce and diced mozzarella. Dust with Parmesan. Repeat layers until pasta sheets are used. Cover top with spaghetti sauce. Dust with remaining Parmesan and layer with slices of mozzarella. Bake uncovered for about 45 minutes or until mozzarella bubbles.

* 9 sheets fresh lasagne, pg. 16
1 tablespoon canola oil
1 large yellow onion, diced
3 cloves garlic, minced
* 2 cups mashed roasted eggplant, pg. 27
1/4 cup chopped fresh flat-leaf parsley
2 cups ricotta cheese
1 cup mashed tofu
* 3 cups spaghetti sauce, pg. 30
1 lb. fresh mozzarella cheese, 1/2 diced, 1/2 sliced
1/2 cup grated Parmesan cheese

use:

• pasta dough, pg. 16
• roasted eggplant, pg. 27
• tomato sauce, pg. 30

MAKES 8 SERVINGS

A two-tone, layered lasagne spruces up a mid-week lull.

tomato pesto lasagne

Heat the oven to 350°. Boil water in a large pot. Add pasta and cook until just tender. Drain and toss with oil to prevent sticking. Grease a small casserole or baking dish. In a small bowl, combine ricotta and egg. Whisk to blend and add salt and pepper. Lay a sheet of pasta on the bottom of casserole. Coat with a layer of tomato pesto. Spoon ricotta mixture on pesto and top with a layer of Gorgonzola. Add remaining pasta sheet and repeat layering until sheets and layering ingredients are used. Layer top with sliced mozzarella. Bake for about 30 minutes, or until mozzarella bubbles.

* 6 sheets fresh lasagne, pg. 16
1 tablespoon canola oil
1 cup ricotta cheese
1 egg
salt and pepper to taste
* $1/2$ cup tomato pesto, pg. 21
$1/4$ cup crumbled Gorgonzola cheese
$1/2$ lb. mozzarella cheese, sliced

use:
- pasta dough, pg. 16
- tomato pesto, pg. 21

MAKES 4 SERVINGS

Forget about ordering Chinese tonight – not when you have the know-how to create these noodles at home.

cold sesame noodles

In a large pot, boil water and cook pasta until tender, about 3 minutes; drain. In a bowl, whisk remaining ingredients until thoroughly combined. Add cool noodles to sesame mixture and toss to coat well. Cover and refrigerate for several hours. Serve on individual plates and garnish with sesame seeds.

* 1 lb. fresh pasta, pg. 16
1 cup tahini
2 tablespoons cider or rice wine vinegar
1 teaspoon minced garlic
1 teaspoon minced fresh ginger
3 tablespoons canola oil
2-3 teaspoons chili oil, or to taste
1-2 tablespoons sugar, or to taste
3 green onions, chopped
salt and pepper to taste
sesame seeds for garnish

MAKES 4 SERVINGS

use:

• pasta dough, pg. 16

Heavy on the Gorgonzola. Heavy on the ham.
This crepe is not for those with delicate constitutions.

ham and Gorgonzola crepes

In a saucepan, gently heat ham, Gorgonzola cream sauce, peas and red pepper. Remove from heat. Spoon some ham mixture into the center of each crepe and roll to close. Transfer to individual plates. Garnish with parsley and a dusting of paprika. Serve immediately.

* 2 cups diced ham, pg. 44
* 2 cups Gorgonzola cream sauce, pg. 29
1/4 cup cooked peas
1/4 cup drained, diced roasted red peppers
* 8 crepes, pg. 18
parsley sprigs for garnish
paprika for dusting

use:

• crepes, pg. 18

• Gorgonzola cream sauce, pg. 29

• honey-mustard glazed ham, pg. 44

MAKES 4 SERVINGS

The sweet acidic flavor of summertime fruit
penetrates this meaty steak filling.

steak and citrus salsa crepes

In a saucepan over medium heat, warm steak and salsa. Spoon steak mixture into center of each crepe and roll to close. Garnish with an orange slice. Serve immediately.

* 2 cups thinly sliced steak, pg. 42
* 1 cup citrus salsa, pg. 23
* 8 crepes, pg. 18
orange slices for garnish

use:

• crepes, pg. 18

• sunny citrus salsa, pg. 23

• honey-mustard steaks, pg. 42

MAKES 4 SERVINGS

You might think you're in Switzerland
after a bite or two of one of these.

Gruyère crepes

In a medium saucepan, heat oil. Add mushrooms and sauté. Add milk. In a small bowl, mix a few spoonfuls of chicken broth with flour to make a slurry. Combine all of stock and add to milk mixture. Stir until thickened. Add cheese to saucepan and stir until completely incorporated. Add chicken, broccoli and carrots. Season to taste. Spoon chicken mixture into the center of each crepe. Fold sides down. Sprinkle with parsley. Serve immediately.

2 tablespoons canola oil
$1/2$ cup sliced fresh mushrooms
2 cups milk
1 cup chicken broth
$1/4$ cup flour
$1/2$ cup grated Gruyère cheese
* 2 cups cubed cooked chicken, pg. 49
$1/2$ cup cooked broccoli florets
$1/4$ cup diced cooked carrots
salt and pepper to taste
* 8 crepes, pg. 18
chopped fresh flat-leaf parsley for garnish

use:
• crepes, pg. 18
• roasted chicken, pg. 49

MAKES 4 SERVINGS

This makes a quick light supper, if you have crepes stored in the freezer. Remove them as soon as you get to the kitchen as they will take about a half hour to defrost.

lumberjack crepes

Brown sausages in a skillet until thoroughly cooked. Drain on paper towels. Heat maple syrup in a small saucepan. Add butter and melt. Place 1 or 2 sausages in the middle of each crepe. Fold sides down. Remove syrup from heat and whisk to blend butter and syrup. Pour syrup over crepes. Dust lightly with confectioners' sugar. Serve immediately.

4 breakfast sausages
1 cup maple syrup
2 tablespoons butter
* 8 crepes, pg. 18
confectioners' sugar

MAKES 4 SERVINGS

use:
• crepes, pg. 18

Take advantage of the autumn months when apples and pears are at their peak.

autumn orchard crepes

Combine sugar, cinnamon, lemon juice, apples, pears and walnuts in a medium saucepan. Add apple juice or water. Cover and simmer over low heat until fruit is tender, about 1 hour. Remove cover and continue cooking to reduce liquid. When mixture has thickened, remove from heat and cool slightly. Spoon some fruit mixture into the center of each crepe. Fold sides down. Top with a dollop of whipped cream or yogurt. Dust with a bit of cinnamon. Serve immediately.

2 tablespoons sugar
$1/4$ teaspoon cinnamon
dash lemon juice, optional
1 cup sliced apples
1 cup sliced pears
$1/4$ cup chopped walnuts
1 tablespoon raisins
$1/2$ cup apple juice or water
* 8 crepes, pg. 18
$1/2$ cup whipped cream or yogurt
cinnamon for dusting

MAKES 4 SERVINGS

use:
• crepes pg. 18

One of life's simple pleasures is picking berries.

berry patch crepes

In a small bowl, combine sugar and orange juice. Stir to dissolve. In another bowl, beat cream cheese until soft. Gradually beat in orange juice mixture. Place berries in a bowl and dust with sugar. Spoon berry mixture into center of each crepe. Spoon cream cheese mixture over berries. Fold sides of crepe down. Spoon berries over top. Garnish with fresh mint leaves. Cover and refrigerate for about 30 minutes.

$1/4$ cup sugar plus 1 tablespoon
   for dusting berries
1 cup orange juice
4 oz. cream cheese or Neufchâtel
   cheese, room temperature
2 cups mixed berries (raspberries,
   blueberries, strawberries)
* 8 crepes, pg. 18
fresh mint leaves for garnish

MAKES 4 SERVINGS

use:

• crepes, pg. 18

Try to find tree-ripe peaches at the height of the season. They will be fragrant and sweet.

peach crepes

In a medium saucepan, combine peaches, orange juice, orange zest, cloves and sugar. Simmer over low heat until mixture becomes syrupy. Remove from heat and remove cloves. Spoon peach mixture onto each crepe and fold sides in. Drizzle a little syrup on top. Garnish with a dollop of whipped cream and berries.

4 ripe peaches, peeled and thinly sliced
1 cup fresh orange juice
1 tablespoon minced orange zest
8 whole cloves
$1/4$ cup sugar
* 8 crepes, pg. 18
whipped cream, optional
$1/4$ cup fresh berries

MAKES 4 SERVINGS

use:
• crepes, pg. 18

Blintzes, like bagels, came to America with the Jewish immigrants at the turn of the century and immediately were adopted by the rest of the population because they are so good.

fruit blintzes

Place fruit in a large bowl. Stir in sugar, lemon juice and mint. Cover and let rest. Transfer cottage cheese to a food processor workbowl . Process until smooth. Add sugar and lemon zest and process until just combined. Spoon cottage cheese mixture into the center of a crepe to make a packet. Fold all sides in. Heat butter in a skillet. Place blintz seam-side down and sauté until golden brown. Carefully turn over and brown lightly. Spoon fruit mixture over blintzes and serve.

2 cups sliced fresh fruit (blueberries, peaches, melon, kiwi)
2 tablespoons sugar
1 teaspoon lemon juice
4 fresh mint leaves, sliced
1$\frac{1}{2}$ cups cottage cheese
2 tablespoons sugar, or to taste
zest of $\frac{1}{2}$ lemon, chopped
* 8 crepes, pg. 18
2 tablespoons butter

MAKES 4 SERVINGS

use:

• crepes, pg. 18

index

index

index